The TRAIN YOUR BRAIN WORKOUT

156 PUZZLE CHALLENGES FOR A STRONGER MIND

PETER DE SCHEPPER AND FRANK COUSSEMENT

imagine!

10 9 8 7 6 5 4 3 2 1

An Imagine Book
Published by Charlesbridge
85 Main Street
Watertown, MA 02472
617-926-0329
www.charlesbridge.com

Illustrations © 2014 PeterFrank t.v.
Cover design by Melissa Gerber

Printed in China, March 2014

ISBN 978-1-62354-040-1

For information about custom editions, special sales, premium and corporate purchases, please contact Charlesbridge Publishing, Inc., at specialsales@charlesbridge.com.

Do brainteasers or computer games have a positive impact on brain activity?

The answer is a resounding "yes." For the last fifteen years we have known that the brain is elastic and it remains so until late in life. Its structure develops constantly as a reaction to your experiences. The more your brain is stimulated, the better your mental condition will be.

An active brain is a better brain.

Proverbial wisdom says "a healthy mind in a healthy body." So you are in control of at least part of this equation. Tests have shown that physical exertion stimulates neurogenesis: those who exercise make significantly more brain cells, which are also granted a longer life. More brain cells ensure better brainpower and better long-term memory.

Brain sport at its best.

This book offers a huge variety of puzzles that will exercise your brain. The puzzles test logical insight, the ability to concentrate, and memory and knowledge. Puzzle-solving will not give you a super brain, but you will learn skills for remembering things better and give certain brain activities an extra boost. If you can't solve certain puzzles, don't look up the answers—just try again later. Finding the solution is much more fun than knowing the solution.

1. Word Search

Word searches are one of the most popular types of puzzles. The object of this puzzle is to find and mark all the hidden words inside the grid. The words may be hidden horizontally, vertically or diagonally, in both directions. The letters that remain unused form a key word when read in reading direction.

Hints:
An efficient method for finding the words is to go through the puzzle per column and look for the first letter of the word. If you find one, then look at the surrounding letters to see if the next letter is there. Do this until you find the whole word. Another useful strategy is to look for words with double letters or letters that are highly noticeable such as Q, X, and Z.

2. Sudoku

The classic Sudoku with a 9x9 grid is still the most popular one. These completely irresistible, totally addictive puzzles offer a fun challenge that keeps fans entertained for hours. All of our Sudokus can be solved by using logic and were created using human logarithms. You should never have to guess what figure to use.

3. Anagrams

Rearrange the letters of a word or phrase to produce a new word or phrase, using all the original letters exactly once; for example "give her two" can be rearranged into "overweight." Extra letters are already in the right place.

4. Letter Blocks

Move the letter blocks around to form words on top and below that you can associate with a theme. In some puzzles, on one or two blocks, the letter from the top row has been switched with the letter from the bottom row.

5. Brainteasers

To solve our brainteasers you must think logically. Use one or several strategies such as direction, differences and/or similarities, associations, calculations, order, spatial insight, colors, quantities, and distances. Our brainteasers ensure that all of the brain's capacities are utilized.

6. Golf Mazes

Start at the cell with a ball and a number on it. Then draw the shortest route from the ball to the hole, the only square without a number. You can only move along vertical and horizontal lines, but not along diagonals. The figure on each square indicates the number of squares the ball must move in the same direction. You can change directions at each stop.

Hint:
Start at the hole and try to find the cell from where you can reach the hole, and then start from the ball.

7. One Letter Less or More
The word below contains the letters of the word above plus or minus the letter in the middle. One letter is already in the right place.

8. Binairo®

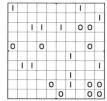

Hey, puzzle fans, get ready for a great new number challenge: Binairo®. These puzzles are just as simple and challenging as Sudoku, but that is where the similarity ends.

Just fill in the grid until there are five zeros and five ones in every row and every column. You can't have more than two of the same number next to or under each other, or have two identical rows or columns.

Hints:
Look for duos of the same number and put the other number before and behind it. Try to avoid trios by entering a zero between two ones or a one between two zeros. Don't forget to count: if you already have five zeros in a row or column, fill in the rest with ones.

9. Word Pyramid
Each word in the pyramid has the letters of the word above it, plus a new letter.

Hints:
Work your way down from top to bottom. If you can't solve a word, skip the line and try to solve the next one.

10. Doodle Puzzle
A doodle puzzle is a combination of images, letters, and/or numbers that indicate a word or a concept.

Hints:
If you cannot solve a doodle puzzle, do not look at the answer right away but come back later. Try to think outside the box.

11. Find the Word

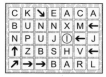 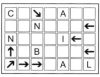

Knowing that every arrow points to a letter and that no letter can touch another vertically, horizontally, or diagonally, find the missing letters that form a key word when read in order. We show one letter in a circle to help you get started.

Hint:
Cross out all letters that surrounding a letter that you have found.

12. Connect

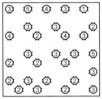 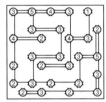

Link all circles with straight horizontal or vertical lines into one connected group. The numbers tell how many lines are connected to a circle. There can be no more than two lines in the same direction and lines cannot cross circles or other lines.

Hints:
A one cannot connect to another one. A two cannot have two connections to another two. A three in a corner must have at least one connection in each direction. A four in a corner has two connections in each direction. A five at the edge must have at least one connection in each direction. A six at the edge has two connections in each direction. A seven in the middle must have at least one connection in each direction. An eight in the middle has two connections in each direction.

So your challenge is to give your brain the best workout it can have, and every one of these puzzles will do that. Enjoy the challenge.

Medium

AUTUMN
COLD
FLOOD
FORECAST
HOT
HURRICANE
PRESSURE
RADIO
RAIN
SNOW
STORM
SUMMER
SUNNY
SUNRISE
WARM

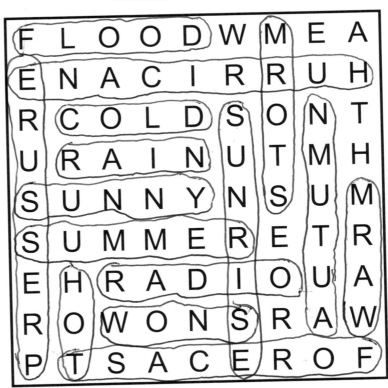

```
F L O O D W M E A
E N A C I R R U H
R C O L D S O N T
U R A I N U T M H
S U N N Y N S U M
S U M M E R E T R
E H R A D I O U A
R O W O N S R A W
P T S A C E R O F
```

All the words are hidden vertically, horizontally, or diagonally, in both directions. The letters that remain unused form a key word when read in order.

WEATHER

Easy

3	5	9	6	2	1	7	8	4
2	4	7	5	8	3	6	1	9
8	6	1	4	9	7	3	2	5
5	3	2	9	1	8	4	7	6
7	8	4	2	5	6	9	3	1
1	9	6	3	7	4	8	5	2
6	7	8	1	4	2	5	9	3
4	1	5	7	3	9	2	6	8
9	2	3	8	6	5	1	4	7

*Fill in the grid so that each row, each column,
and each 3x3 frame contains every number from 1 to 9.*

Medium

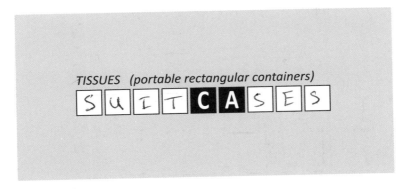

TISSUES   (portable rectangular containers)

S U I T **C A** S E S

COME OVER SIR   (delivers food and drink to guests)

R O O M S E R V I C E

Form the word or phrase that is described in parentheses with the letters above the grid. Extra letters are already in the right place.

Easy

Solution

Move the letter blocks around to form words on top
and below that you can associate with **sports**.

Medium

ICEBERG 5

Which iceberg (1–6) lacks a penguin?

Medium

	5	4	3	5	2
3	4	3	3	2	5
1	2	2	3	4	4
1	1	2	1	4	3
2	1	4	1	3	1
3	5	5	3	1	1

Draw the shortest path from the ball to the hole. You can only move along vertical and horizontal lines. The figure on each square indicates the number of squares the ball must move in the same direction. You can change direction at each stop.

Hard

The word below contains the letters of the word
above plus or minus the letter in the middle.
One letter is already in the right place.

Easy

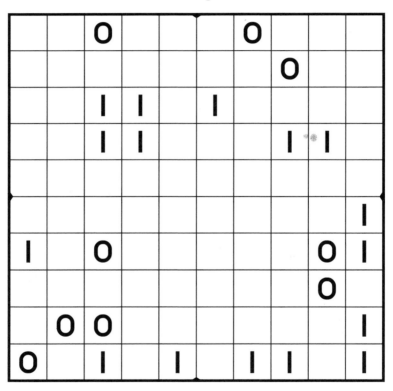

Complete the grid with zeros and ones until there are five zeros and five ones in every row and every column. No more than two of the same number can be next to or under each other. Rows or columns with exactly the same content are not allowed.

WORD PYRAMID

Medium

(1) expresses position

(2) furry, domesticated mammal

(3) informal conversation

(4) betray

(5) Swiss house

(6) honorable

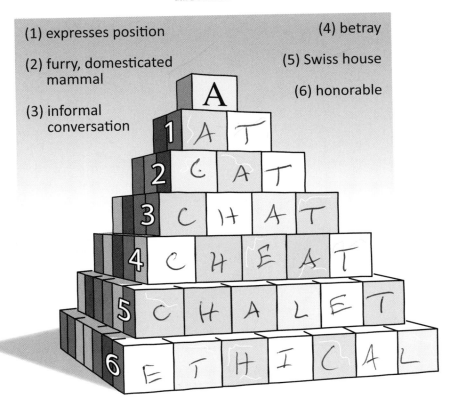

*Each word in the pyramid has the letters of
the word above it, plus a new letter.*

Easy

$$\frac{SP}{SOR}$$

*What word or concept
is depicted here?*

SPONSOR

Easy

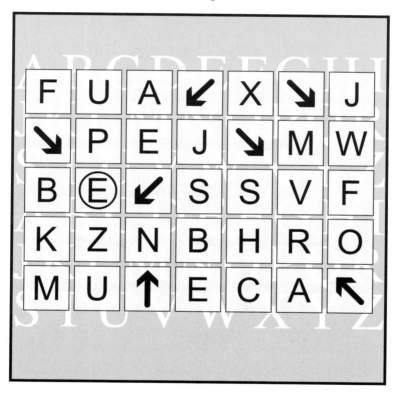

*Knowing that every arrow points to a letter and that no letter
can touch another vertically, horizontally, or diagonally, find
the missing letters that form a key word when read in order.
We show one letter in a circle to help you get started.*

Easy

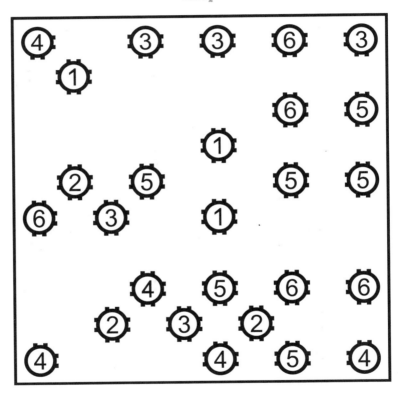

Link all circles with straight horizontal or vertical lines into one connected group. The numbers tell how many lines are connected to a circle. There can be no more than two lines in the same direction and lines cannot cross circles or other lines.

Medium

BATH
CHAIR
DOOR
FOOD
GLASS
HANDLE
HATSTAND
RETRO
SHELF
SINK
SOFA
STEEL
STOOL
STORAGE
TABLE
TRENDY
WOOD

Y	D	N	E	R	T	E	F	S
H	T	A	B	S	U	L	R	T
A	F	O	S	F	S	B	H	E
T	R	S	T	O	R	A	G	E
S	N	O	O	O	N	T	L	L
T	W	R	O	D	I	T	U	G
A	O	T	L	D	K	N	I	S
N	O	E	R	C	H	A	I	R
D	D	R	S	H	E	L	F	E

*All the words are hidden vertically, horizontally,
or diagonally, in both directions. The letters that remain
unused form a key word when read in order.*

Medium

9	8	7	4	6		5	3	
3	1	6	8			4	7	
2	5	4				6	8	
6	2	3	7	1	8	9	4	5
74	74	1	5			8	6	2
5	8	9		4	6	1	1	7
1	6	5	2	8	7	3	9	4
37	379	8			4	1	2	6
134	349	2				7	5	8

Fill in the grid so that each row, each column,
and each 3x3 frame contains every number from 1 to 9.

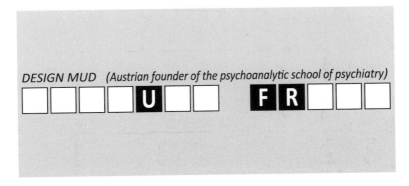

Medium

DESIGN MUD *(Austrian founder of the psychoanalytic school of psychiatry)*

| | | | **U** | | | **F** | **R** | | | |

MINOR *(Narcotic extracted from opium used to relieve pain)*

| | | | **P** | **H** | | | **E** |

Form the word or phrase that is described in parentheses with the letters above the grid. Extra letters are already in the right place.

Medium

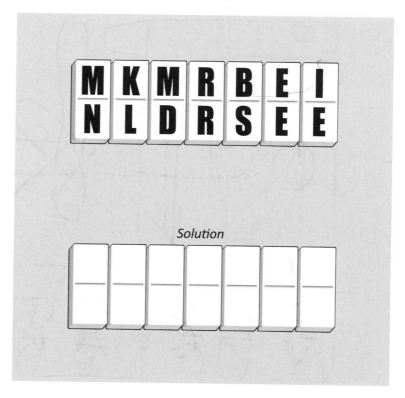

Solution

Move the letter blocks around to form words on top and
below that you can associate with **kitchenware**.
The letters are reversed on one block.

Very Hard

Which ski (1–7) does not belong?

Medium

2	1	4	4	2	3
2	3	3	2	2	1
1	2	1	2	2	2
5	4	3	3	4	5
2	4	4	2	1	5
	1	1	4	1	3

Draw the shortest path from the ball to the hole. You can only move along vertical and horizontal lines. The figure on each square indicates the number of squares the ball must move in the same direction. You can change direction at each stop.

Hard

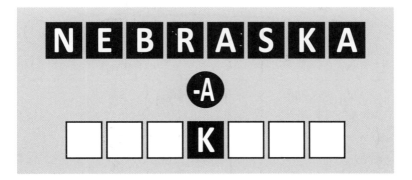

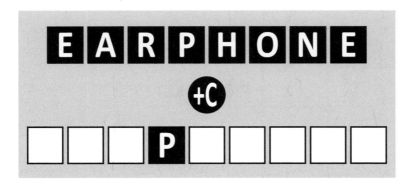

The word below contains the letters of the word
above plus or minus the letter in the middle.
One letter is already in the right place.

Medium

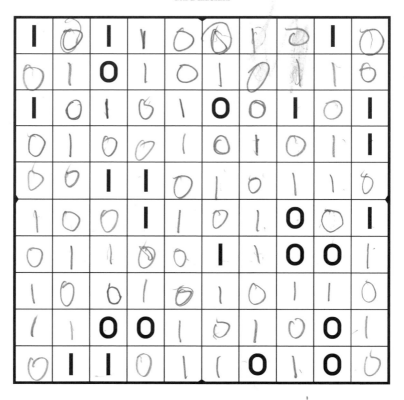

Complete the grid with zeros and ones until there are five zeros and five ones in every row and every column. No more than two of the same number can be next to or under each other. Rows or columns with exactly the same content are not allowed.

WORD PYRAMID

Medium

(1) to ... or not

(2) place to sleep

(3) liability

(4) introduction

(5) broken

(6) slowest

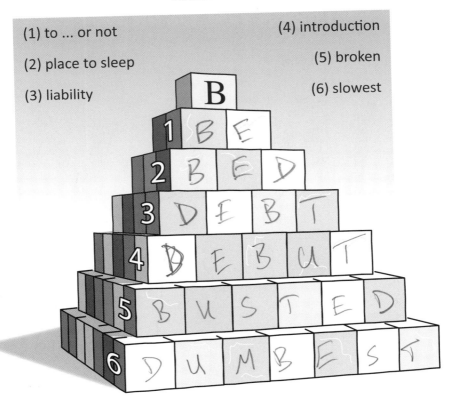

Each word in the pyramid has the letters of
the word above it, plus a new letter.

Medium

*What word or concept
is depicted here?*

Medium

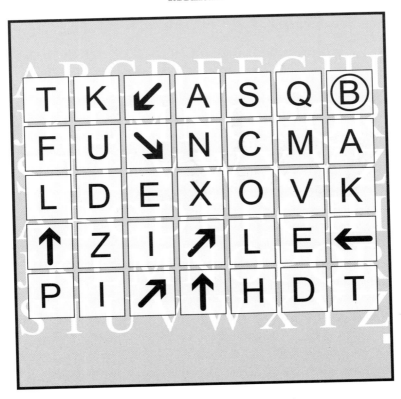

T	K	↙	A	S	Q	Ⓑ
F	U	↘	N	C	M	A
L	D	E	X	O	V	K
↑	Z	I	↗	L	E	←
P	I	↗	↑	H	D	T

Knowing that every arrow points to a letter and that no letter can touch another vertically, horizontally, or diagonally, find the missing letters that form a key word when read in order. We show one letter in a circle to help you get started.

Hard

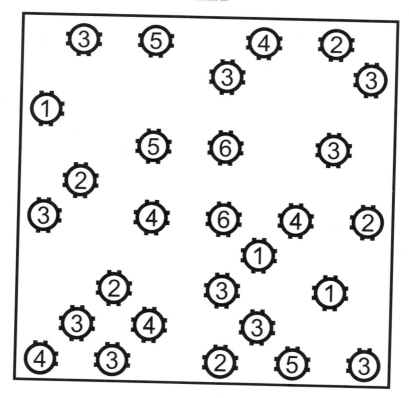

Link all circles with straight horizontal or vertical lines into one connected group. The numbers tell how many lines are connected to a circle. There can be no more than two lines in the same direction and lines cannot cross circles or other lines.

WORD SEARCH

Medium

BITE
CRICKET
DAMAGE
DISEASES
EARWIG
FIREFLY
HONEYBEE
MAGGOT
MAYFLY
SCARAB
SPIDER
STING
TERMITE

*All the words are hidden vertically, horizontally,
or diagonally, in both directions. The letters that remain
unused form a key word when read in order.*

31

Hard

2	5	6	8	1	7	4	3	9
4	1	8	6	9	3	7	5	2
3	9	7	2	4	5	8	6	1
9	6	5	7	2	8	1	4	3
7	3	1	9	5	4	2	8	6
8	2	4	3	6	1	9	7	5
1	8	9	5	7	6	3	2	4
6	7	2	4	3	9	5	1	8
5	4	3	1	8	2	6	9	7

*Fill in the grid so that each row, each column,
and each 3x3 frame contains every number from 1 to 9.*

Medium

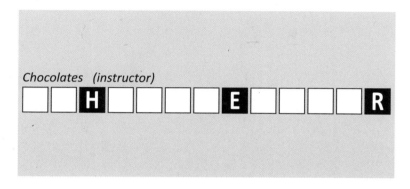

Chocolates (instructor)

| | | H | | | | E | | | | R |

No stream (a clever communication device)

| | | | | | P | H | | | |

Form the word or phrase that is described in parentheses with the letters above the grid. Extra letters are already in the right place.

Hard

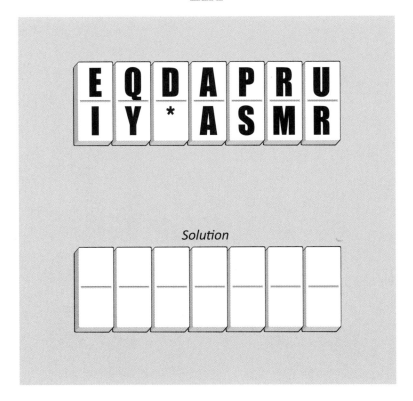

Solution

Move the letter blocks around to form words on top
and below that you can associate with **shapes**.
The letters are reversed on two blocks.

Hard

Which digit should replace the question mark in the score?

Medium

1	5	3	4	4	4
1	2		4	2	1
4	3	3	1	4	4
4	2	1	3	4	2
1	2	4	3	1	4
2	1	5	4	1	2

Draw the shortest path from the ball to the hole. You can only move along vertical and horizontal lines. The figure on each square indicates the number of squares the ball must move in the same direction. You can change direction at each stop.

Hard

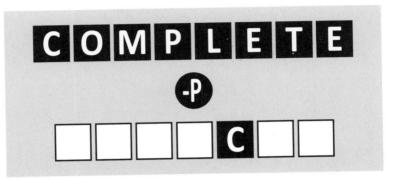

The word below contains the letters of the word above plus or minus the letter in the middle. One letter is already in the right place.

Hard

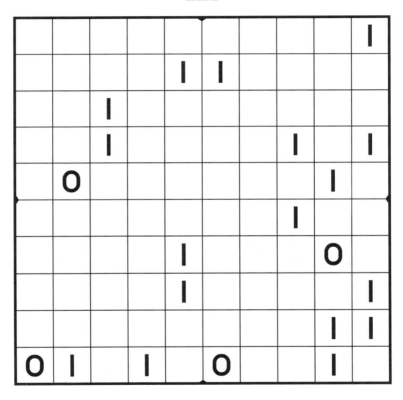

Complete the grid with zeros and ones until there are five zeros and five ones in every row and every column. No more than two of the same number can be next to or under each other. Rows or columns with exactly the same content are not allowed.

Medium

(1) electric current

(2) curve

(3) black-and-white toothed whale

(4) nocturnal insect

(5) performed by a choir

(6) intestinal infection caused by ingestion

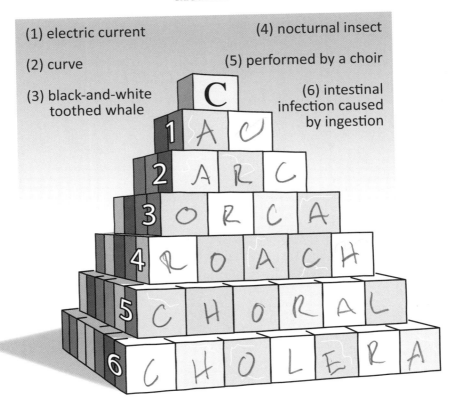

1. A C
2. A R C
3. O R C A
4. R O A C H
5. C H O R A L
6. C H O L E R A

Each word in the pyramid has the letters of the word above it, plus a new letter.

Medium

$$\frac{CLOUD}{TH}$$

*What word or concept
is depicted here?*

Hard

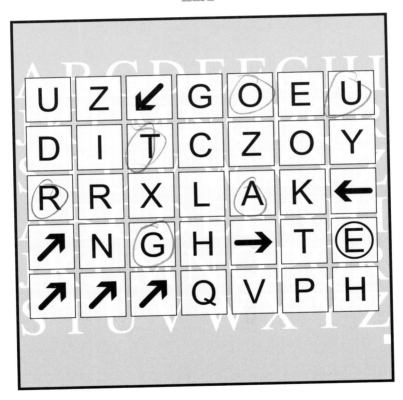

U	Z	↙	G	O	E	U
D	I	T	C	Z	O	Y
R	R	X	L	A	K	←
↗	N	G	H	→	T	E
↗	↗	↗	Q	V	P	H

Knowing that every arrow points to a letter and that no letter can touch another vertically, horizontally, or diagonally, find the missing letters that form a key word when read in order. We show one letter in a circle to help you get started.

OUTRAGE

Hard

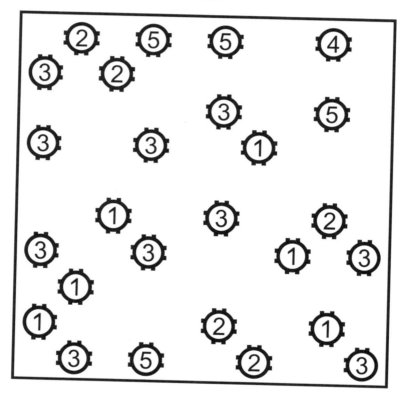

Link all circles with straight horizontal or vertical lines into one connected group. The numbers tell how many lines are connected to a circle. There can be no more than two lines in the same direction and lines cannot cross circles or other lines.

Medium

BATHE
CANAL
DRINK
DROWN
FLOAT
FLOOD
FLOW
FOOD
FOUNTAIN
OASIS
RAIN
SALT
SHIP
SHOWER
SINK
SNOW
SPOUT
STREAM
WASH

F	L	O	A	T	R	A	I	N
P	B	W	A	E	H	O	I	S
I	A	C	W	S	S	A	L	T
H	T	O	A	I	T	S	D	R
S	H	W	O	N	S	I	R	E
S	E	F	U	K	A	S	I	A
D	O	O	L	F	T	L	N	M
E	F	S	P	O	U	T	K	R
F	O	O	D	N	W	O	R	D

All the words are hidden vertically, horizontally, or diagonally, in both directions. The letters that remain unused form a key word when read in order.

Very Hard

						6	2	
					5		3	9
1				4			9	
		7	3					1
		2	7		8			5
	1					9		
2	9	8				1		
			6				7	8

*Fill in the grid so that each row, each column,
and each 3x3 frame contains every number from 1 to 9.*

Medium

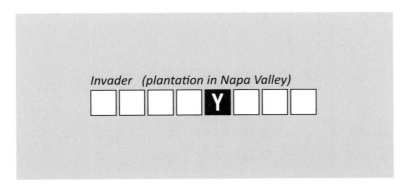

Invader   *(plantation in Napa Valley)*

| | | | | Y | | | |

Rituals   *(country and continent)*

| | | | | | A | | | A |

Form the word or phrase that is described in parentheses with the letters above the grid. Extra letters are already in the right place.

Easy

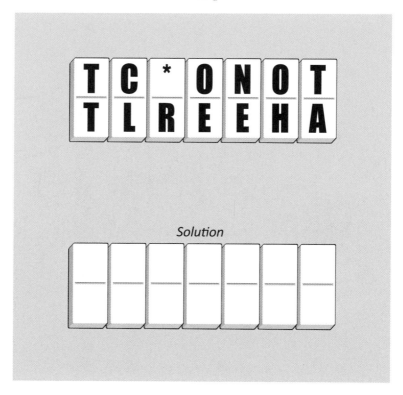

Solution

*Move the letter blocks around to form words on top
and below that you can associate with **clothes**.*

Medium

*From how many different cakes
do these pieces originate?*

4+2=6

Medium

1	4	5	5	(4)	4
2	4	4	2	4	2
4	1	3	2	4	4
1	4	2	3	●	5
1	2	1	4	3	3
3	4	3	5	4	3

Draw the shortest path from the ball to the hole. You can only move along vertical and horizontal lines. The figure on each square indicates the number of squares the ball must move in the same direction. You can change direction at each stop.

Hard

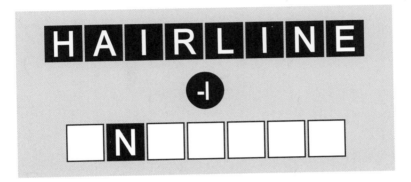

The word below contains the letters of the word above plus or minus the letter in the middle. One letter is already in the right place.

Easy

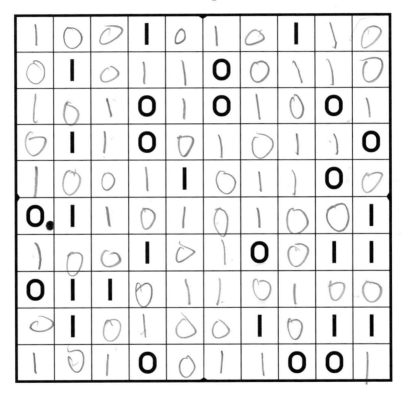

Complete the grid with zeros and ones until there are five zeros
and five ones in every row and every column. No more than two
of the same number can be next to or under each other. Rows
or columns with exactly the same content are not allowed.

Medium

(1) one tenth of a meter

(2) dense

(3) female domestic

(4) tools used to store and deliver information

(5) crown

(6) looked up to

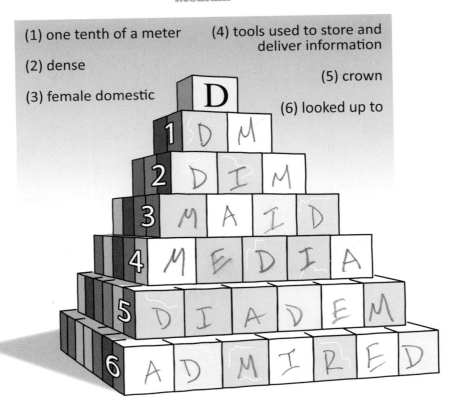

1	D	M			
2	D	I	M		
3	M	A	I	D	
4	M	E	D	I	A
5	D	I	A	D	E	M
6	A	D	M	I	R	E	D

*Each word in the pyramid has the letters of
the word above it, plus a new letter.*

DOODLE PUZZLE

Medium

Airline

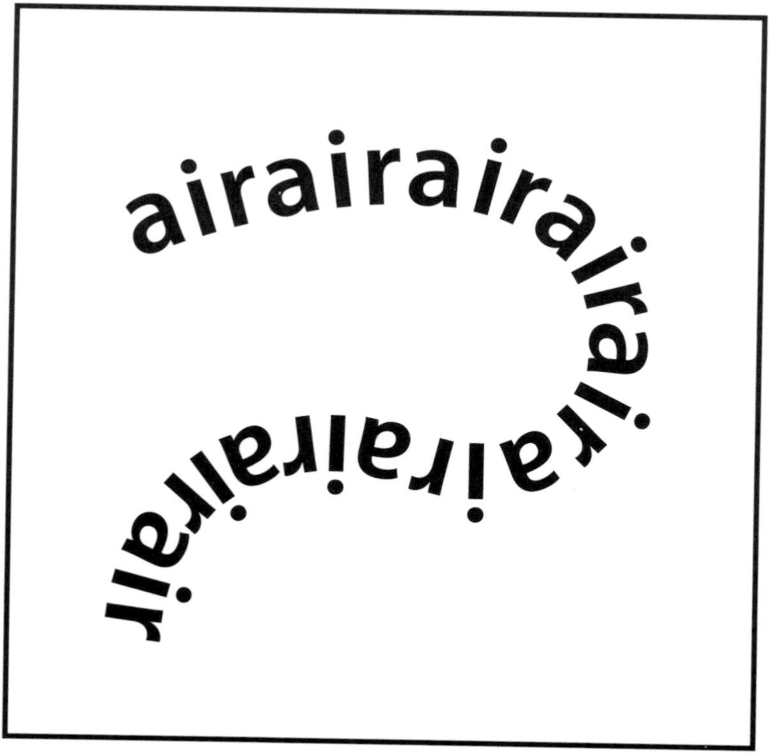
airairairairairairairairair

What word or concept is depicted here?

Easy

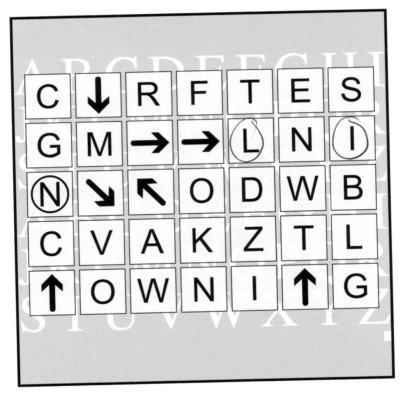

Knowing that every arrow points to a letter and that no letter can touch another vertically, horizontally, or diagonally, find the missing letters that form a key word when read in order. We show one letter in a circle to help you get started.

Easy

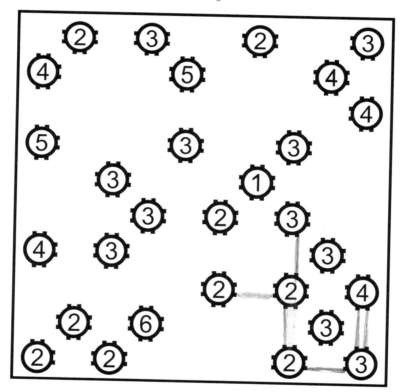

Link all circles with straight horizontal or vertical lines into one connected group. The numbers tell how many lines are connected to a circle. There can be no more than two lines in the same direction and lines cannot cross circles or other lines.

Medium

BANKING
BANNER
BLOG
CABLE
CHAT
CRASH
FILE
MODEM
MOUSE
PORTAL
PROTOCOL
SERVER
SURF
UPLOAD
VIRUS

H	S	G	O	L	B	I	E	N
S	U	F	T	A	H	C	L	M
A	R	I	T	E	R	N	B	E
R	I	L	U	P	L	O	A	D
C	V	E	A	M	F	E	C	O
L	O	C	O	T	O	R	P	M
B	A	N	N	E	R	U	U	T
R	E	V	R	E	S	O	S	S
G	N	I	K	N	A	B	P	E

All the words are hidden vertically, horizontally, or diagonally, in both directions. The letters that remain unused form a key word when read in order.

Easy

4						5	6	
6	5	1	2	4	3	7	8	9
			5		6		3	
5		6	1	2		3	4	8
2	1	8	6	3	4	9	7	5
	4	3	8		5		2	
				8			9	
				1				2
		7						

Fill in the grid so that each row, each column,
and each 3x3 frame contains every number from 1 to 9.

Medium

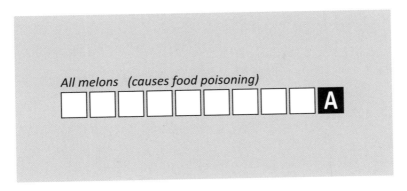

All melons   (causes food poisoning)

| | | | | | | | | | A |

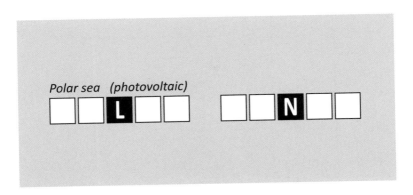

Polar sea   (photovoltaic)

| | | L | | | | | N | |

Form the word or phrase that is described in parentheses with the letters above the grid. Extra letters are already in the right place.

Medium

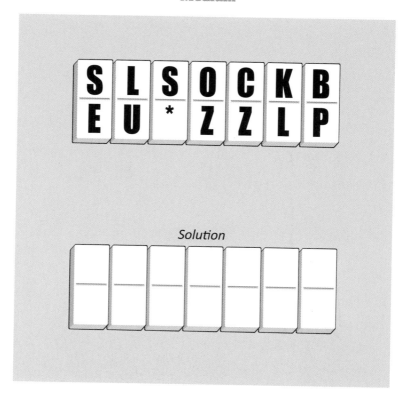

Solution

Move the letter blocks around to form words on top
and below that you can associate with **toys**.
The letters are reversed on one block.

Medium

Which two letters are missing in the conversation between the two Venetian carnival merrymakers?

GOLF MAZE

Medium

2	1	3	4	5	2
5	2	4	2	2	5
4	2	3	2	1	4
4	3	2	3	4	1
3	3	1	3	2	
3	1	5	2	3	2

Draw the shortest path from the ball to the hole. You can only move along vertical and horizontal lines. The figure on each square indicates the number of squares the ball must move in the same direction. You can change direction at each stop.

60

Hard

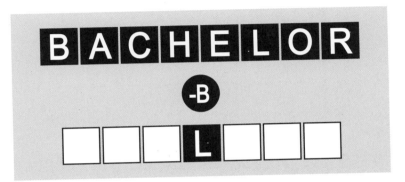

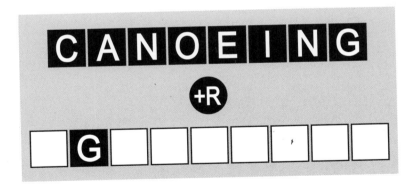

*The word below contains the letters of the word
above plus or minus the letter in the middle.
One letter is already in the right place.*

BINAIRO®

Medium

								I	O
O		O							
					O		I		I
									I
		I	I						
							O		I
		O	O						I
		O	O				O		
I					I		O	O	
	I	I						O	

Complete the grid with zeros and ones until there are five zeros
and five ones in every row and every column. No more than two
of the same number can be next to or under each other. Rows
or columns with exactly the same content are not allowed.

62

WORD PYRAMID

Medium

(1) compass point

(2) group of things

(3) animal refuge

(4) small picture inserted within the bounds of a larger one

(5) game

(6) vivid

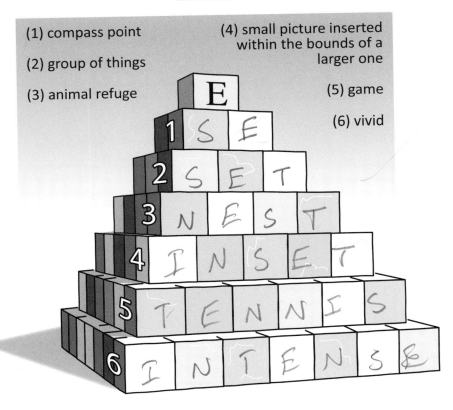

		E			
1	S	E			
2	S	E	T		
3	N	E	S	T	
4	I	N	S	E	T
5	T	E	N	N	I	S
6	I	N	T	E	N	S	E

*Each word in the pyramid has the letters of
the word above it, plus a new letter.*

Hard

5 down
4 down
3 down
2 down
1 down

*What word or concept
is depicted here?*

FIND THE WORD

Medium

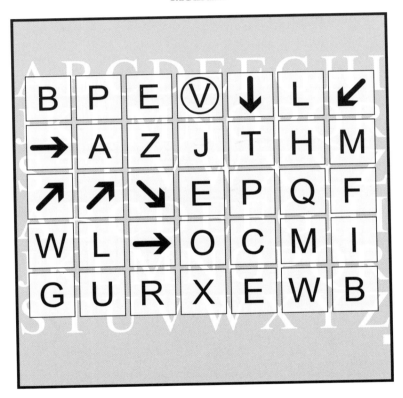

*Knowing that every arrow points to a letter and that no letter
can touch another vertically, horizontally, or diagonally, find
the missing letters that form a key word when read in order.
We show one letter in a circle to help you get started.*

Medium

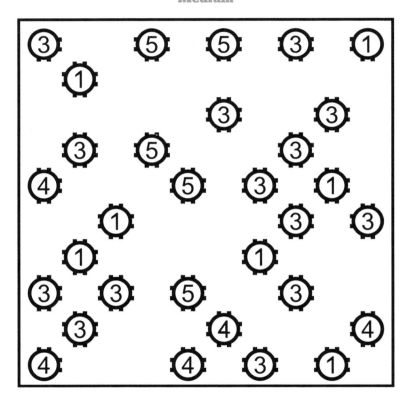

Link all circles with straight horizontal or vertical lines into one connected group. The numbers tell how many lines are connected to a circle. There can be no more than two lines in the same direction and lines cannot cross circles or other lines.

Medium

ARTERY

BLOOD

DIARRHEA

DOCTOR

FLU

HERNIA

MEASLES

OXYGEN

RETINA

SHINGLES

VACCINE

VIRUS

WOMB

S	E	L	S	A	E	M	D	B
H	H	E	R	N	I	A	I	L
V	A	C	C	I	N	E	A	O
E	A	D	O	C	T	O	R	O
F	O	X	Y	G	E	N	R	D
L	S	E	L	G	N	I	H	S
U	R	E	T	I	N	A	E	L
A	R	T	E	R	Y	T	A	H
B	M	O	W	V	I	R	U	S

All the words are hidden vertically, horizontally,
or diagonally, in both directions. The letters that remain
unused form a key word when read in order.

Medium

				5	7			
		4					8	
		1	8		6			
	5		4				9	7
4		7		2	5			
		5		3			4	
7		2		6	4			8
1		9	5		8		3	6

*Fill in the grid so that each row, each column,
and each 3x3 frame contains every number from 1 to 9.*

68

Medium

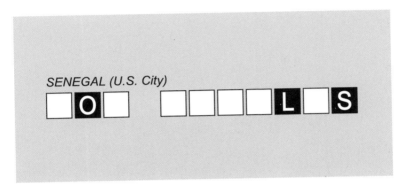

SENEGAL *(U.S. City)*

☐ **O** ☐   ☐ ☐ ☐ ☐ **L** ☐ **S**

CANNOT CUT *(someone who audits businesses)*

A ☐ ☐ ☐ ☐ ☐ ☐ ☐ ☐ ☐

Form the word or phrase that is described in parentheses with the letters above the grid. Extra letters are already in the right place.

Hard

Solution

Move the letter blocks around to form words on top
and below that you can associate with the **garden**.
The letters are reversed on two blocks.

Hard

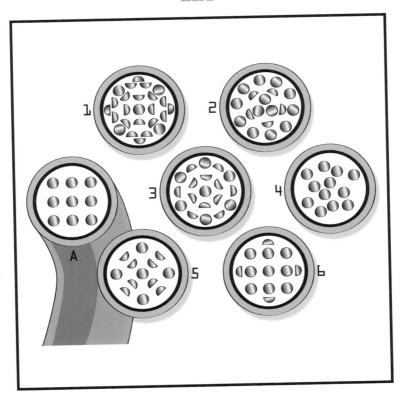

*Fiberglass cable A, with nine glass fibers,
cannot pass on the largest quantity of light signals.
Which fiberglass cable (1–6) can do that?*

Medium

2	1	5	1	4	1
3	1	4	1	3	1
1	1	1	0	1	1
5	2	3	3	2	4
5	4	4	4	3	5
	5	4	3	1	0

Draw the shortest path from the ball to the hole. You can only move along vertical and horizontal lines. The figure on each square indicates the number of squares the ball must move in the same direction. You can change direction at each stop.

Hard

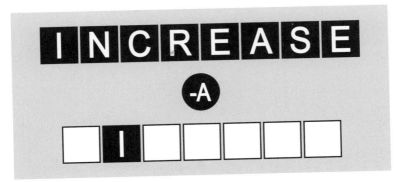

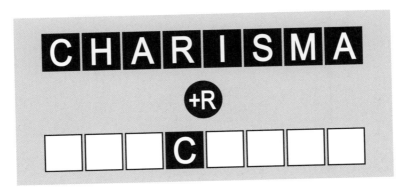

*The word below contains the letters of the word
above plus or minus the letter in the middle.
One letter is already in the right place.*

Hard

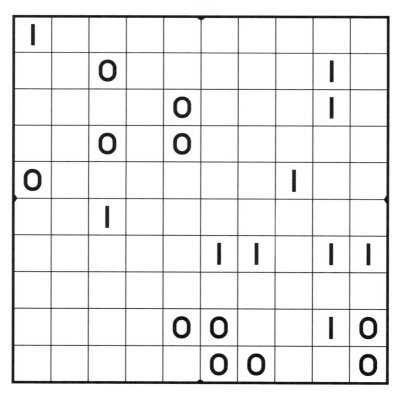

Complete the grid with zeros and ones until there are five zeros and five ones in every row and every column. No more than two of the same number can be next to or under each other. Rows or columns with exactly the same content are not allowed.

Medium

(1) musical note

(2) plump

(3) quick

(4) realities

(5) workmanships

(6) elements

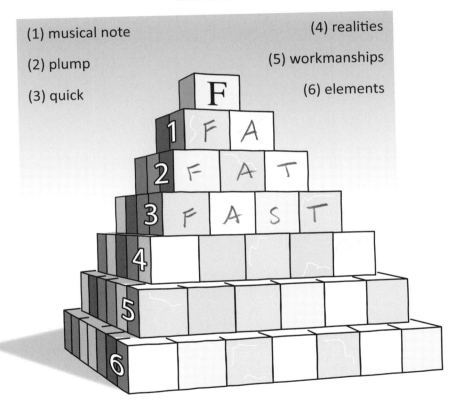

Each word in the pyramid has the letters of the word above it, plus a new letter.

Medium

*What word or concept
is depicted here?*

Hard

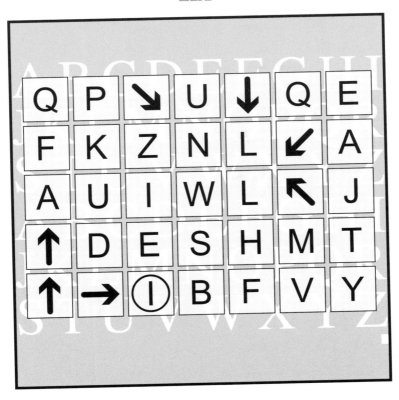

Knowing that every arrow points to a letter and that no letter can touch another vertically, horizontally, or diagonally, find the missing letters that form a key word when read in order. We show one letter in a circle to help you get started.

Hard

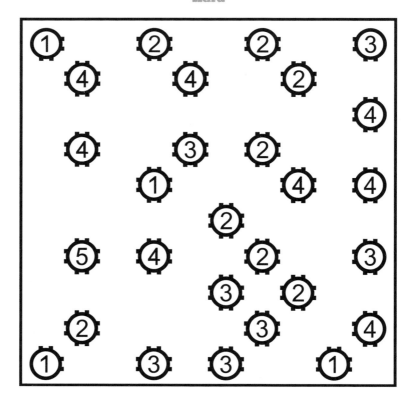

Link all circles with straight horizontal or vertical lines into one connected group. The numbers tell how many lines are connected to a circle. There can be no more than two lines in the same direction and lines cannot cross circles or other lines.

Medium

ANIMALS

ECOLOGY

EROSION

EXTINCT

FAUNA

FLORA

HEALTH

KYOTO

MANURE

RECYCLING

REPORT

TIDES

```
Y G O L O C E E N
N N V A N U A F O
T I D E S I R O I
O L H T L A E H S
T C N I T X E N O
O Y M T R O P E R
Y C M A N U R E E
K E A N I M A L S
E R N F L O R A T
```

All the words are hidden vertically, horizontally, or diagonally, in both directions. The letters that remain unused form a key word when read in order.

79

Hard

			4	5				
3			4	5				
4		9		3				
			8			1		
					6	5		
	3	8					4	
9				7	3	6	8	
	6		9					1
		1		4			5	

*Fill in the grid so that each row, each column,
and each 3x3 frame contains every number from 1 to 9.*

80

Medium

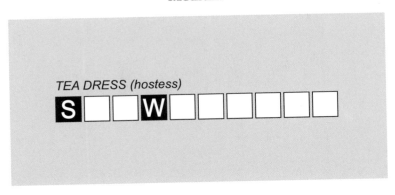

TEA DRESS (hostess)

| S | | | W | | | | | |

NORDIC ALP (major part of the central nervous system)

| S | | | | | | | | | |

Form the word or phrase that is described in parentheses with the
letters above the grid. Extra letters are already in the right place.

Easy

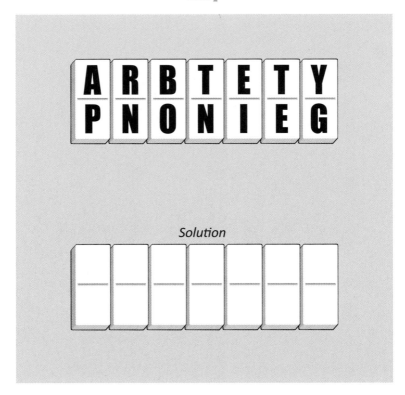

Solution

*Move the letter blocks around so that words are formed on top and below that you can associate with **chess**.*

Hard

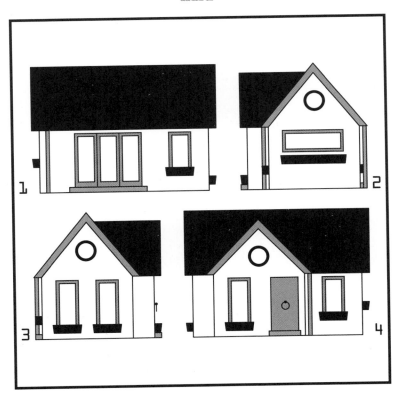

At which angle (1–4) of this house is an element missing?

Medium

4	5	1	5	5	2
1	4	4	1	2	5
2	1	2	3	4	4
3	4	2		0	3
5	4	4	3	1	5
3	1	3	1	3	1

Draw the shortest path from the ball to the hole. You can only
move along vertical and horizontal lines. The figure on each
square indicates the number of squares the ball must move in
the same direction. You can change direction at each stop.

84

Hard

*The word below contains the letters of the word
above plus or minus the letter in the middle.
One letter is already in the right place.*

Easy

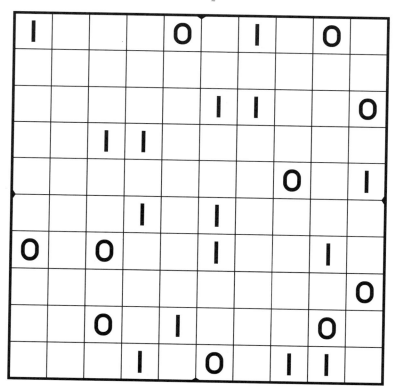

Complete the grid with zeros and ones until there are five zeros
and five ones in every row and every column. No more than two
of the same number can be next to or under each other. Rows
or columns with exactly the same content are not allowed.

Medium

(1) as an example

(2) acquire

(3) movable barrier in a fence

(4) broker

(5) feeding

(6) time of origin

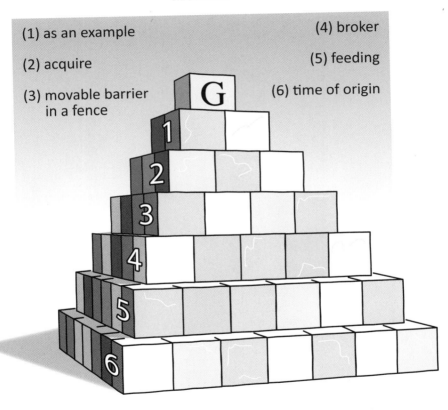

Each word in the pyramid has the letters of the word above it, plus a new letter.

Medium

*What word or concept
is depicted here?*

Easy

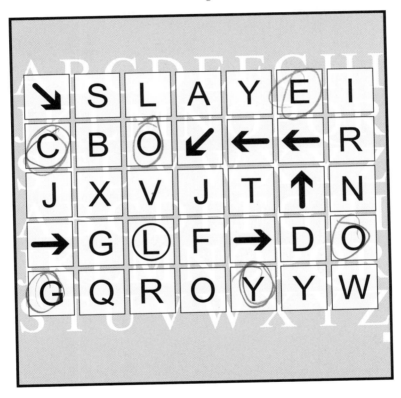

Knowing that every arrow points to a letter and that no letter
can touch another vertically, horizontally, or diagonally, find
the missing letters that form a key word when read in order.
We show one letter in a circle to help you get started.

ECOLOGY

Easy

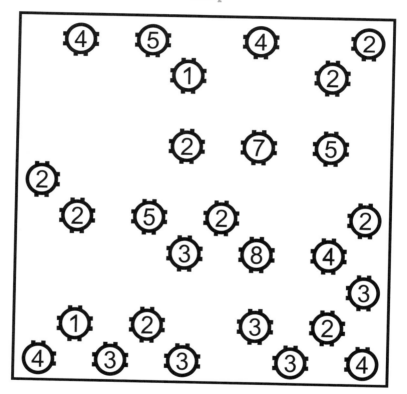

Link all circles with straight horizontal or vertical lines into one connected group. The numbers tell how many lines are connected to a circle. There can be no more than two lines in the same direction and lines cannot cross circles or other lines.

Medium

ANOLIS
CARNIVORE
COBRA
CRAWL
DERMIS
FROG
GECKO
IGUANA
LAND
LEECH
LUNGS
SCALES
SEA SNAKE
TOADS
VENOM

O	S	T	O	A	D	S	R	E
D	K	G	A	N	O	L	I	S
L	E	C	N	A	P	V	C	C
E	T	R	E	U	I	E	O	A
E	L	E	M	G	L	N	B	L
C	A	R	N	I	V	O	R	E
H	F	R	O	G	S	M	A	S
L	W	A	R	C	L	A	N	D
S	E	A	S	N	A	K	E	S

All the words are hidden vertically, horizontally, or diagonally, in both directions. The letters that remain unused form a key word when read in order.

Very Hard

							8	
5				6	1			
	1	3	2	5				
	5							6
1		8		3	9	7	2	
7				8			3	
						9		
		5	8	9		3		
			7		3			

*Fill in the grid so that each row, each column,
and each 3x3 frame contains every number from 1 to 9.*

Medium

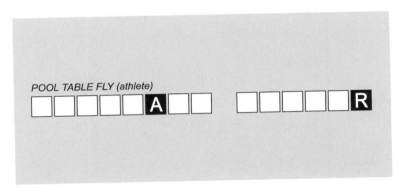

POOL TABLE FLY *(athlete)*

⬜⬜⬜⬜⬜**A**⬜⬜   ⬜⬜⬜⬜⬜**R**

MISCALLED *(intermediate socioeconomic position)*

⬜⬜⬜**D**⬜⬜   ⬜⬜⬜⬜**S**

Form the word or phrase that is described in parentheses with the letters above the grid. Extra letters are already in the right place.

Medium

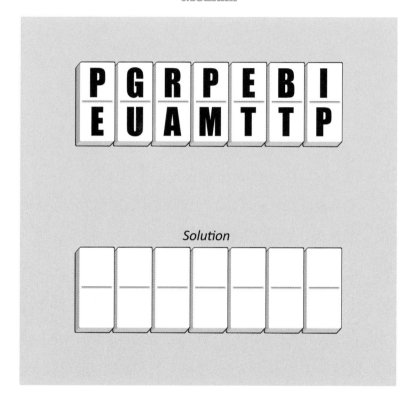

Solution

*Move the letter blocks around so that words are formed on top and below that you can associate with **instruments**. The letters were reversed on one block.*

Hard

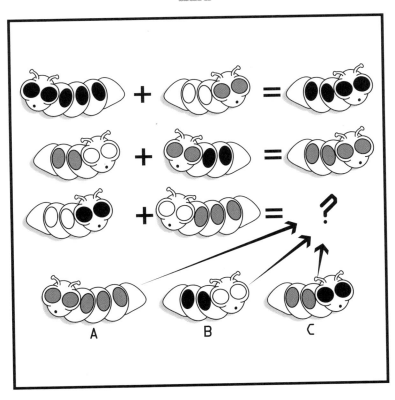

Just like in genetics, dominant colors are at play here.
Which worm (A–C) should replace the question mark?

Medium

	5	5	5	2	1
2	3	1	4	2	1
3	3	0	3	3	2
4	2	3	2	2	5
4	2	4	1	2	1
1	2	1	2	1	2

Draw the shortest path from the ball to the hole. You can only move along vertical and horizontal lines. The figure on each square indicates the number of squares the ball must move in the same direction. You can change direction at each stop.

Hard

*The word below contains the letters of the word
above plus or minus the letter in the middle.
One letter is already in the right place.*

97

Medium

					O				I
								O	O
O		I				I			O
		I		O	O				
							I	I	
		I		O					
				O		O		O	I
		O					I		I
		O				O			
I					O	O			

Complete the grid with zeros and ones until there are five zeros and five ones in every row and every column. No more than two of the same number can be next to or under each other. Rows or columns with exactly the same content are not allowed.

Medium

(1) male

(2) of a female

(3) long-eared mammal

(4) muscular organ

(5) menace

(6) dramatic art

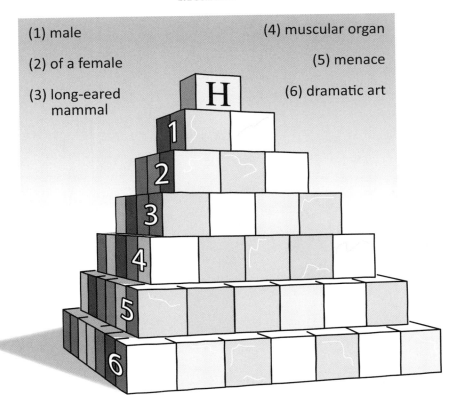

Each word in the pyramid has the letters of the word above it, plus a new letter.

Medium

*What word or concept
is depicted here?*

Medium

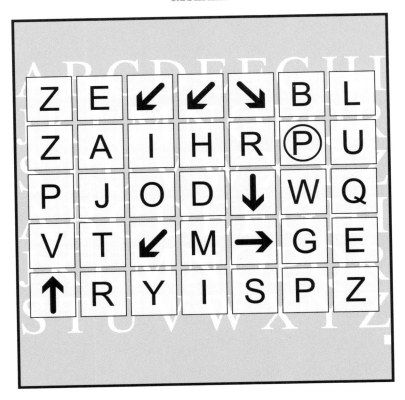

Knowing that every arrow points to a letter and that no letter can touch another vertically, horizontally, or diagonally, find the missing letters that form a key word when read in order. We show one letter in a circle to help you get started.

Medium

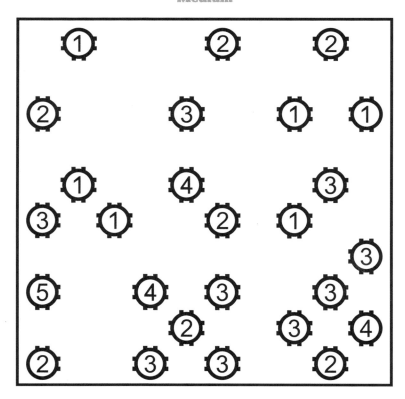

Link all circles with straight horizontal or vertical lines into one connected group. The numbers tell how many lines are connected to a circle. There can be no more than two lines in the same direction and lines cannot cross circles or other lines.

Medium

ABACUS
ADD
AXIOM
BODY
CIRCLE
CONIC
COSINE
DIGIT
EVEN
EXPONENT
LINE
LOGIC
POWER
PROOF
SURFACE

```
E S U R F A C E Y
X L A X I O M M D
P E C R E W O P O
O A N R T V T R B
N C H I I I E E P
E L O M S C G N A
N I A N L O G I C
T N D T I I C C D
S E D S U C A B A
```

*All the words are hidden vertically, horizontally,
or diagonally, in both directions. The letters that remain
unused form a key word when read in order.*

Easy

				3				
3	4		6		5			
		1						5
	1			5				9
9		3	4			8		
		4	2		9	1		3
4	9	6				7	1	8
	3							
	7	8	9	4			2	

*Fill in the grid so that each row, each column,
and each 3x3 frame contains every number from 1 to 9.*

Medium

HERNIA *(cyclone)*

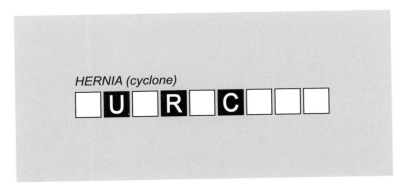

| | U | | R | | C | | | |

BANKERS *(U.S. State)*

| | | | | | | A |

Form the word or phrase that is described in parentheses with the letters above the grid. Extra letters are already in the right place.

Hard

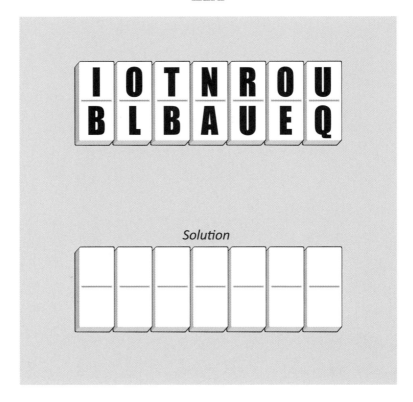

Solution

Move the letter blocks around to form words on top and
below that you can associate with **alcoholic drinks**.
The letters are reversed on two blocks.

Medium

Which bell makes a sound that differs from the other sounds?

Medium

1	4	5	4	2	5
5	2	3	2	3	3
1	4	2	1	4	1
5	4	3	1	3	5
2	1	4	3	2	3
3	1	4	1		3

Draw the shortest path from the ball to the hole. You can only move along vertical and horizontal lines. The figure on each square indicates the number of squares the ball must move in the same direction. You can change direction at each stop.

Hard

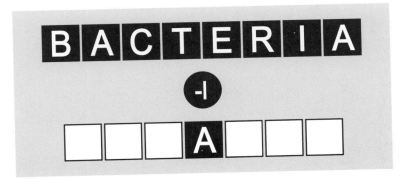

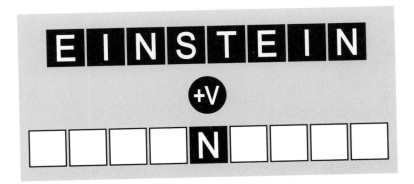

The word below contains the letters of the word above plus or minus the letter in the middle. One letter is already in the right place.

109

Hard

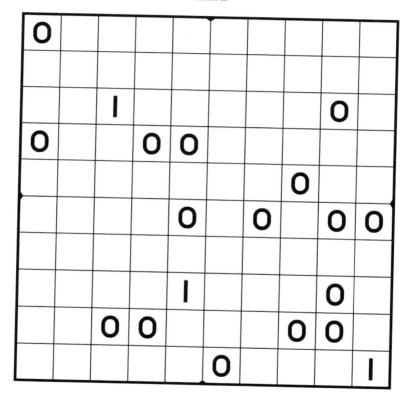

Complete the grid with zeros and ones until there are five zeros
and five ones in every row and every column. No more than two
of the same number can be next to or under each other. Rows
or columns with exactly the same content are not allowed.

Medium

(1) Rhode Island

(2) gentle wind

(3) water falling in drops

(4) fairy bluebird

(5) aviators

(6) vivid red

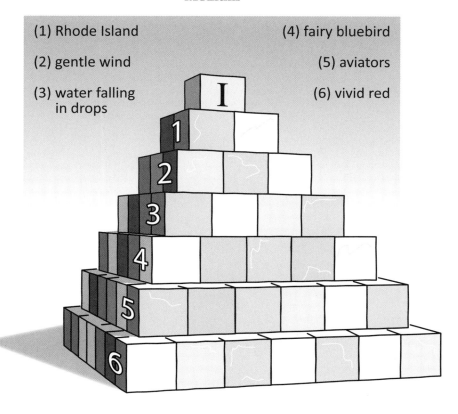

Each word in the pyramid has the letters of the word above it, plus a new letter.

Hard

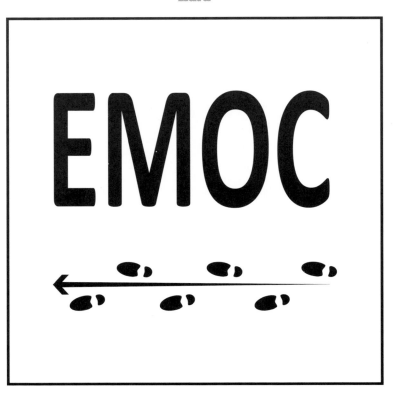

*What word or concept
is depicted here?*

Hard

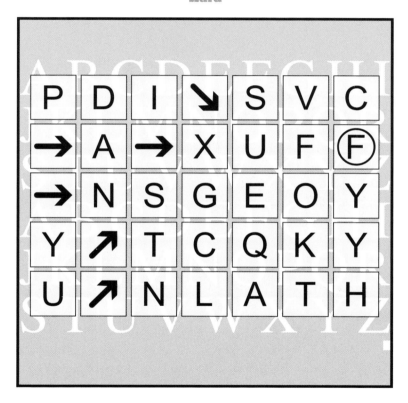

Knowing that every arrow points to a letter and that no letter can touch another vertically, horizontally, or diagonally, find the missing letters that form a key word when read in order. We show one letter in a circle to help you get started.

Hard

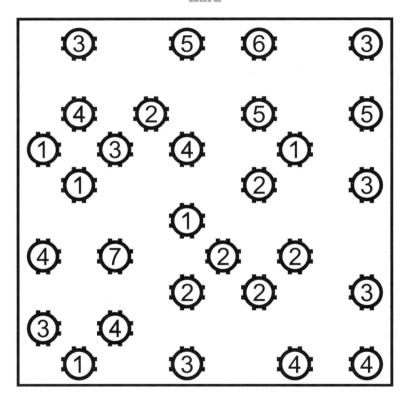

Link all circles with straight horizontal or vertical lines into one connected group. The numbers tell how many lines are connected to a circle. There can be no more than two lines in the same direction and lines cannot cross circles or other lines.

Medium

BARDOT

FARROW

FAWCETT

FONDA

FOSTER

GARBO

GOLDBERG

LOREN

MONROE

ROBERTS

SPACEK

WEAVER

WEISZ

WELCH

R	S	P	A	C	E	K	T	A
G	E	C	T	R	Z	S	T	E
S	O	V	F	O	S	T	E	R
M	B	L	A	S	I	R	C	H
O	A	L	D	E	E	E	W	C
N	R	O	N	B	W	B	A	L
R	D	R	O	E	E	O	F	E
O	O	E	F	A	R	R	O	W
E	T	N	O	B	R	A	G	S

All the words are hidden vertically, horizontally, or diagonally, in both directions. The letters that remain unused form a key word when read in order.

Medium

2					1	6	8	
	6		8	5	2			
8	4		7		9	2	5	1
7			9		6	3		2
	1							
9				8	3			
4			1	9				
		2						
						5	7	

*Fill in the grid so that each row, each column,
and each 3x3 frame contains every number from 1 to 9.*

Medium

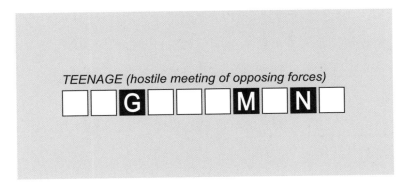

TEENAGE (hostile meeting of opposing forces)

| | | G | | | | M | | N | |

PROTESTER (police officer)

| | | A | | | | T | | O | | | |

Form the word or phrase that is described in parentheses with the letters above the grid. Extra letters are already in the right place.

Easy

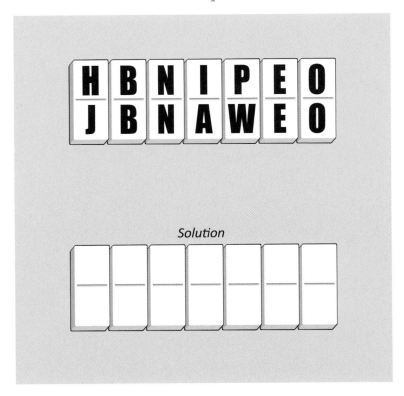

Solution

*Move the letter blocks around to form words on top and below that you can associate with **bones**.*

Medium

*Which rose (1–6) doesn't belong
to the same family as all the others?*

GOLF MAZE

Medium

3	2	4	4	4	4
2	3	1	2	3	5
2	1	0	1	2	1
4	4	3	3	3	4
1	3	4	1	2	1
2		1	5	5	2

Draw the shortest path from the ball to the hole. You can only move along vertical and horizontal lines. The figure on each square indicates the number of squares the ball must move in the same direction. You can change direction at each stop.

120

Hard

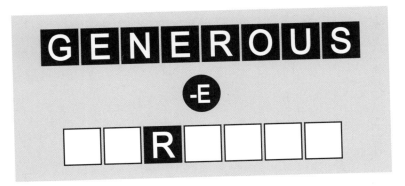

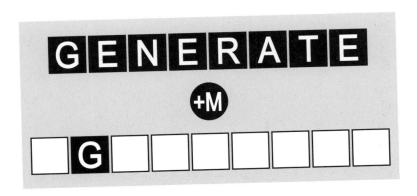

*The word below contains the letters of the word
above plus or minus the letter in the middle.
One letter is already in the right place.*

Easy

				0		0		
0	0	1		1					0
	1	0	0	1		0	1	0	1
	1			0		1		1	0
	0				1	0	0	1	0
	0							0	1
	1			0	1	1	0	0	1
1			0	1	0	0	1	1	0
			1	0	0	1	1	0	0
			1	0	0	1	1	0	0	1

Complete the grid with zeros and ones until there are five zeros
and five ones in every row and every column. No more than two
of the same number can be next to or under each other. Rows
or columns with exactly the same content are not allowed.

Medium

(1) the city of Angels

(2) beer

(3) bargain

(4) 4th letter of the Greek alphabet

(5) individual feature or fact

(6) particular form of a language

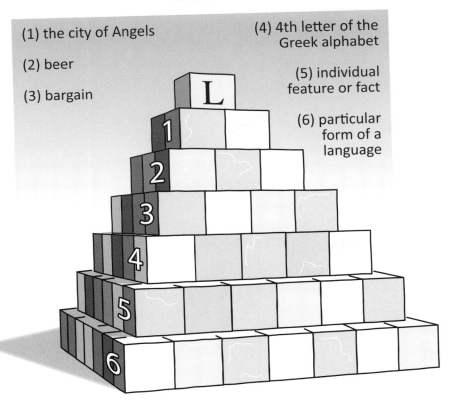

Each word in the pyramid has the letters of the word above it, plus a new letter.

Hard

*What word or concept
is depicted here?*

Easy

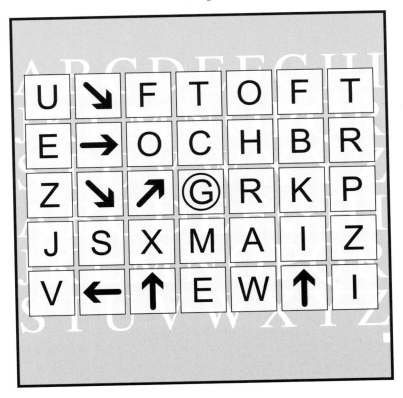

U	↘	F	T	O	F	T
E	→	O	C	H	B	R
Z	↘	↗	Ⓖ	R	K	P
J	S	X	M	A	I	Z
V	←	↑	E	W	↑	I

Knowing that every arrow points to a letter and that no letter can touch another vertically, horizontally, or diagonally, find the missing letters that form a key word when read in order. We show one letter in a circle to help you get started.

Easy

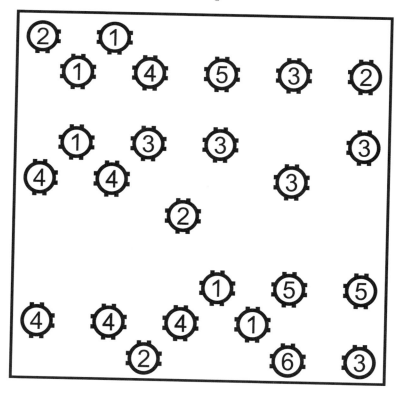

Link all circles with straight horizontal or vertical lines into
one connected group. The numbers tell how many lines are
connected to a circle. There can be no more than two lines in
the same direction and lines cannot cross circles or other lines.

Medium

ARAGORN

BATTLE

BIFUR

BILBO

ELVES

FIELDS

GANDALF

GOLLUM

GONDOR

IRON HILLS

MORDOR

RINGS

STOORS

UMBAR

I	R	O	D	N	O	G	T	O
B	R	F	B	B	I	F	U	R
L	A	O	I	L	K	I	M	E
M	R	T	N	E	I	U	B	L
O	A	R	T	H	L	B	A	V
R	G	I	E	L	I	D	R	E
D	O	N	O	N	E	L	S	S
O	R	G	A	N	D	A	L	F
R	N	S	T	O	O	R	S	S

All the words are hidden vertically, horizontally,
or diagonally, in both directions. The letters that remain
unused form a key word when read in order.

Hard

								1
	3	4						
6	7		8	2				
			3				9	
				7			2	
		8	2				6	4
					8		4	2
1		5						3
7			4					

*Fill in the grid so that each row, each column,
and each 3x3 frame contains every number from 1 to 9.*

Medium

CLIENT (choice)

| E | | | | | | O | |

NEED DIET (sovereign)

| | N | | | P | | | | N | |

Form the word or phrase that is described in parentheses with the letters above the grid. Extra letters are already in the right place.

Medium

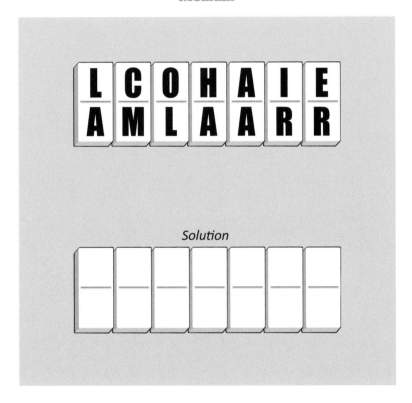

Solution

Move the letter blocks around to form words on top
and below that you can associate with **diseases**.
The letters are reversed on one block.

Medium

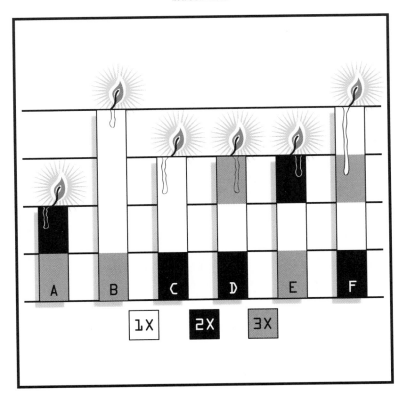

1X 2X 3X

Which candle (A–F) will burn down first, if the black wax burns twice as long, as the white, and the gray wax, three times longer?

Medium

Draw the shortest path from the ball to the hole. You can only move along vertical and horizontal lines. The figure on each square indicates the number of squares the ball must move in the same direction. You can change direction at each stop.

Hard

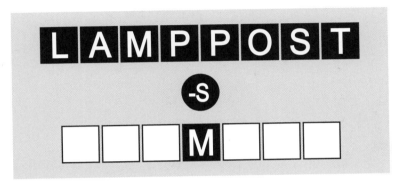

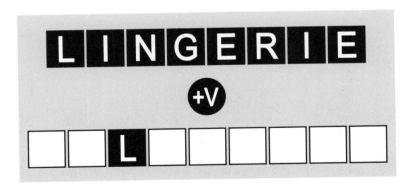

The word below contains the letters of the word above plus or minus the letter in the middle. One letter is already in the right place.

133

Medium

0								0	
	0		0		0				0
				I			0		0
		I	I				0	0	
		I							
	I			0		I		I	I
								I	
		0	0			I			0
I					0				0
		I		I			0		

Complete the grid with zeros and ones until there are five zeros
and five ones in every row and every column. No more than two
of the same number can be next to or under each other. Rows
or columns with exactly the same content are not allowed.

134

Medium

(1) I

(2) large Australian bird

(3) donkey

(4) feather

(5) dock worker

(6) collapse or fold

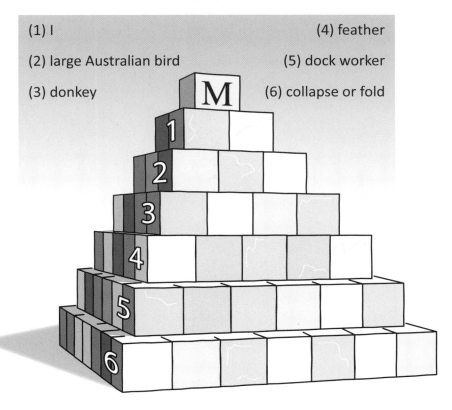

*Each word in the pyramid has the letters of
the word above it, plus a new letter.*

DOODLE PUZZLE

Medium

ZEBRA *What word or concept is depicted here?*

Medium

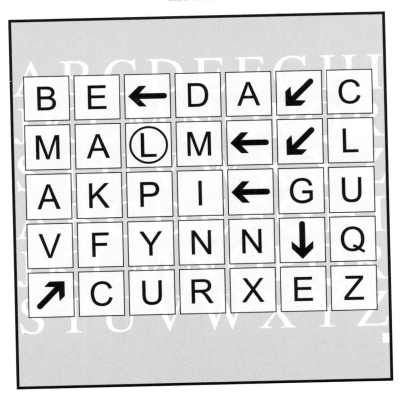

B	E	←	D	A	↙	C
M	A	Ⓛ	M	←	↙	L
A	K	P	I	←	G	U
V	F	Y	N	N	↓	Q
↗	C	U	R	X	E	Z

Knowing that every arrow points to a letter and that no letter can touch another vertically, horizontally, or diagonally, find the missing letters that form a key word when read in order. We show one letter in a circle to help you get started.

Medium

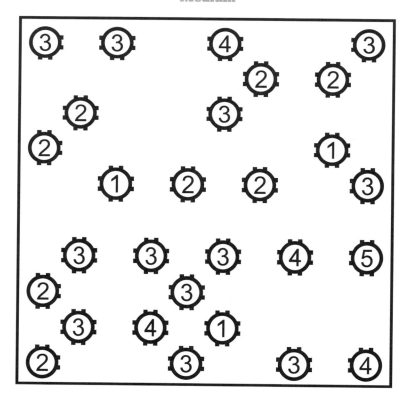

Link all circles with straight horizontal or vertical lines into one connected group. The numbers tell how many lines are connected to a circle. There can be no more than two lines in the same direction and lines cannot cross circles or other lines.

Medium

ASSIST
BACKBOARD
BLOCK
BOUNCE
CHARGE
COACH
GUARD
JOHNSON
JORDAN
MATCH
SCORE
SPORT
STEAL
TEAM
TIE

S	A	S	S	I	S	T	G	E
K	C	B	T	T	A	S	U	C
K	C	O	C	E	I	E	A	N
N	H	O	R	O	A	E	R	U
A	A	M	L	E	A	L	D	O
D	R	A	O	B	K	C	A	B
R	G	T	R	O	P	S	H	T
O	E	C	B	A	T	E	A	M
J	O	H	N	S	O	N	L	L

*All the words are hidden vertically, horizontally,
or diagonally, in both directions. The letters that remain
unused form a key word when read in order.*

Very Hard

					2			
					6		3	
	1						2	8
		9			4	7		
	3							
		1		3	7		8	9
	5	6						7
9						2	1	
		7	5		3			

*Fill in the grid so that each row, each column,
and each 3x3 frame contains every number from 1 to 9.*

Medium

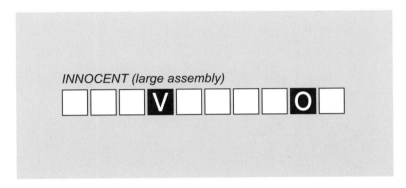

INNOCENT *(large assembly)*

| | | | V | | | | O | |

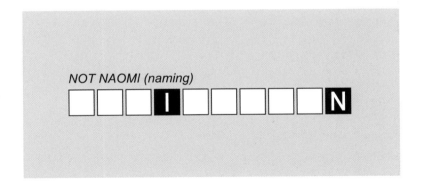

NOT NAOMI *(naming)*

| | | | I | | | | | N |

Form the word or phrase that is described in parentheses with the letters above the grid. Extra letters are already in the right place.

Hard

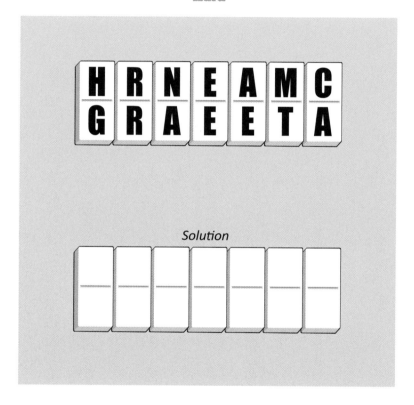

Solution

Move the letter blocks around to form words on top
and below that you can associate with **professions**.
The letters are reversed on two blocks.

Hard

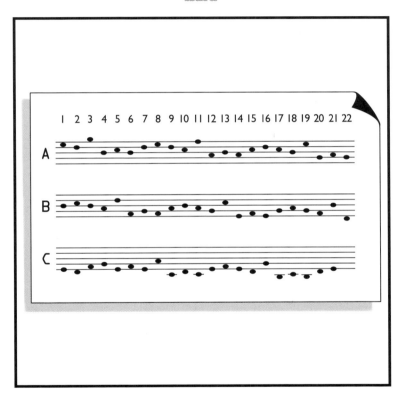

In this score, the same refrain is repeated eight times, but played a tone lower each time. Which note is superfluous? Answer like this: B9.

Medium

2	2	1	2	1	1
3	3	1	2	3	1
3	1	2	1	3	4
5	3	1	0	3	2
1	3	3		3	4
0	1	1	1	4	4

Draw the shortest path from the ball to the hole. You can only move along vertical and horizontal lines. The figure on each square indicates the number of squares the ball must move in the same direction. You can change direction at each stop.

Hard

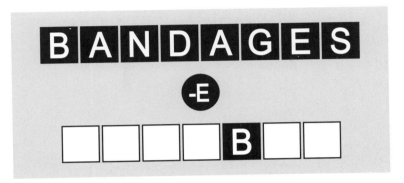

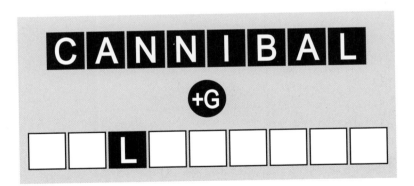

The word below contains the letters of the word above plus or minus the letter in the middle. One letter is already in the right place.

145

Hard

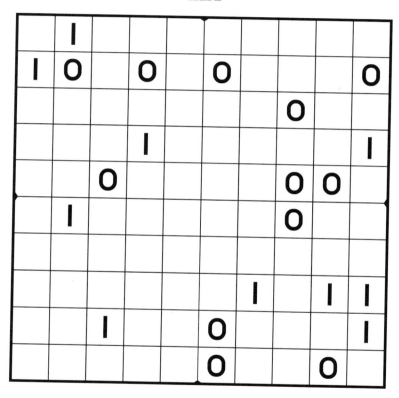

Complete the grid with zeros and ones until there are five zeros and five ones in every row and every column. No more than two of the same number can be next to or under each other. Rows or columns with exactly the same content are not allowed.

Medium

(1) depart

(2) self

(3) box in a theater

(4) sphere

(5) baffle

(6) person who maintains a web log

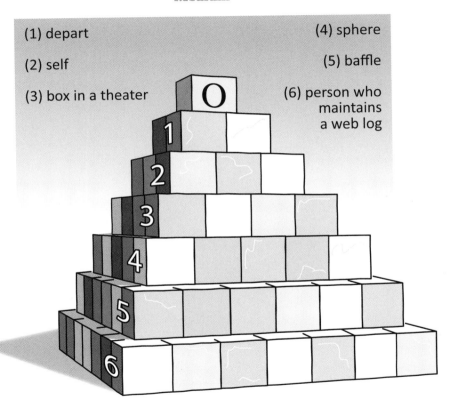

Each word in the pyramid has the letters of the word above it, plus a new letter.

Medium

*What word or concept
is depicted here?*

Hard

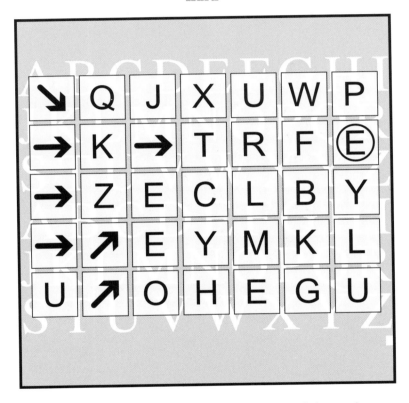

Knowing that every arrow points to a letter and that no letter can touch another vertically, horizontally, or diagonally, find the missing letters that form a key word when read in order. We show one letter in a circle to help you get started.

CONNECT

Hard

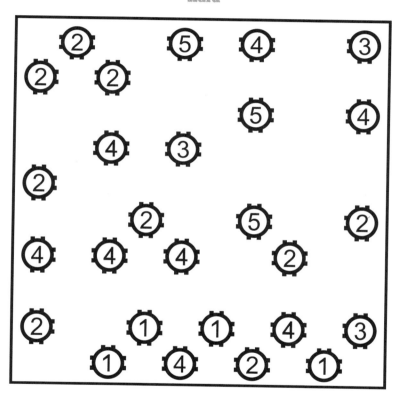

Link all circles with straight horizontal or vertical lines into one connected group. The numbers tell how many lines are connected to a circle. There can be no more than two lines in the same direction and lines cannot cross circles or other lines.

Medium

AWL
CHISEL
DRILL
FILE
FRETSAW
GLOVE
HAMMER
HELMET
INK
JIGSAW
LATHE
NAIL
PUNCH
RULER
TRIANGLE
WRENCH

L	T	G	E	P	U	N	C	H
W	E	L	H	C	N	A	I	L
A	L	O	T	H	H	W	N	W
O	G	V	A	I	A	W	K	A
E	N	E	L	S	M	R	D	S
L	A	O	T	E	M	E	R	G
I	I	E	L	L	E	N	I	I
F	R	U	L	E	R	C	L	J
F	T	E	M	L	E	H	L	S

All the words are hidden vertically, horizontally, or diagonally, in both directions. The letters that remain unused form a key word when read in order.

Easy

	2		1			8	9	
3	1	9			8		7	
	8	5	3		6		2	
	9	3				2	1	7
			4		3		6	
8							4	
				7	2			9
5	4			3				

Fill in the grid so that each row, each column,
and each 3x3 frame contains every number from 1 to 9.

Medium

TUNING *(pursue for food or sport)*

H ☐ ☐ ☐ ☐ ☐ ☐

TART ALARM *(weaponless self-defense)*

☐ ☐ ☐ ☐ I ☐ ☐   ☐ ☐ ☐

Form the word or phrase that is described in parentheses with the letters above the grid. Extra letters are already in the right place.

Easy

Solution

Move the letter blocks around to form words on top
and below that you can associate with **car parts**.

*Which appointment doesn't respect
the logic that the other appointments follow?*

Medium

	2	3	3	5	4
4	2	1	4	1	3
5	1	3	1	2	5
5	2	1	2	3	4
5	2	2	2	4	1
1	4	1	3	2	2

Draw the shortest path from the ball to the hole. You can only move along vertical and horizontal lines. The figure on each square indicates the number of squares the ball must move in the same direction. You can change direction at each stop.

Hard

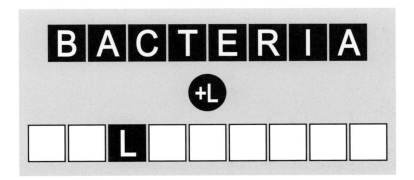

The word below contains the letters of the word
above plus or minus the letter in the middle.
One letter is already in the right place.

Easy

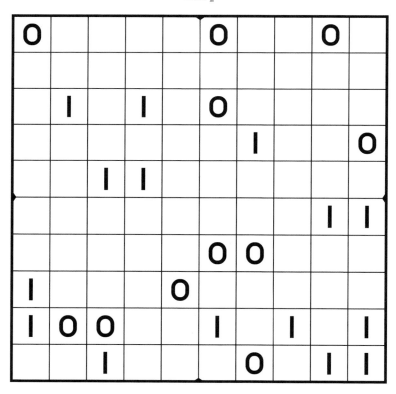

Complete the grid with zeros and ones until there are five zeros and five ones in every row and every column. No more than two of the same number can be next to or under each other. Rows or columns with exactly the same content are not allowed.

Medium

(1) platinum

(2) metal container

(3) secret plan

(4) qualified to fly

(5) cultivated

(6) of the best quality

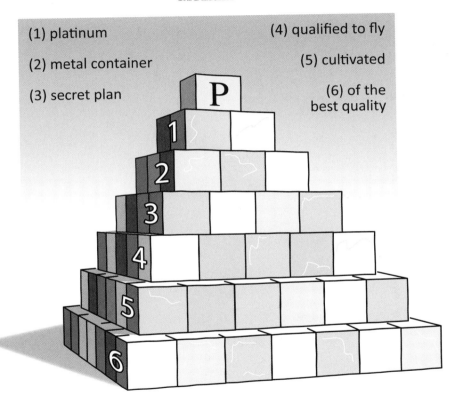

Each word in the pyramid has the letters of the word above it, plus a new letter.

Hard

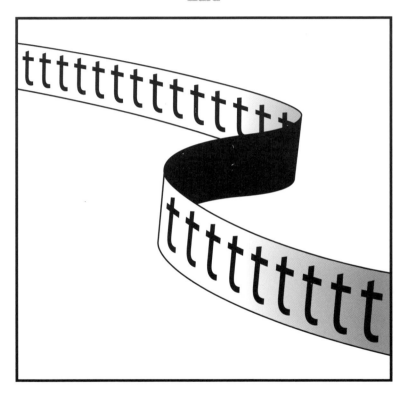

*What word or concept
is depicted here?*

Easy

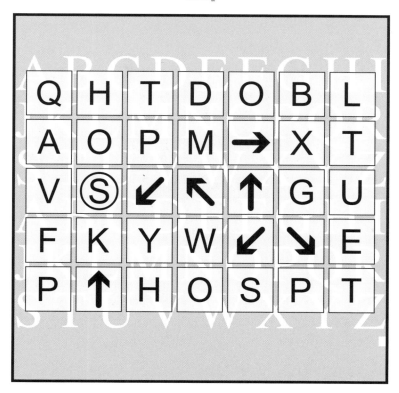

Knowing that every arrow points to a letter and that no letter can touch another vertically, horizontally, or diagonally, find the missing letters that form a key word when read in order. We show one letter in a circle to help you get started.

Easy

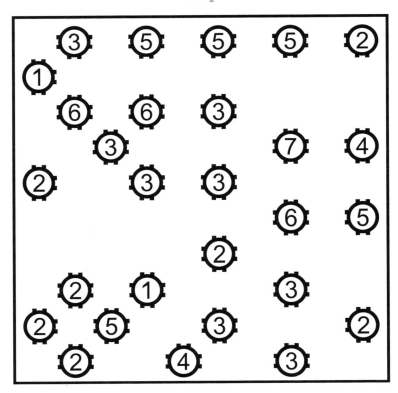

Link all circles with straight horizontal or vertical lines into one connected group. The numbers tell how many lines are connected to a circle. There can be no more than two lines in the same direction and lines cannot cross circles or other lines.

If you can't solve certain puzzles, don't look up the answers— just try again later.

Finding the solution is much more fun than knowing the solution.

page 7
WEATHER

page 8

3	5	9	6	2	1	7	8	4
2	4	7	5	8	3	6	1	9
8	6	1	4	9	7	3	2	5
5	3	2	9	1	8	4	7	6
7	8	4	2	5	6	9	3	1
1	9	6	3	7	4	8	5	2
6	7	8	1	4	2	5	9	3
4	1	5	7	3	9	2	6	8
9	2	3	8	6	5	1	4	7

page 9
SUITCASES
ROOM SERVICE

page 10
SWIMMING
BASEBALL

page 11
Iceberg 5. Penguins only live on icebergs with a circular opening.

page 12

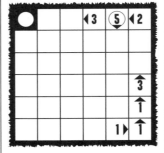

page 13
BLAMING
PREDATORS

page 14

I	I	0	0	I	0	0	I	I	0
I	I	0	0	I	0	I	0	I	0
0	0	I	I	0	I	I	0	0	I
0	0	I	I	0	I	0	I	I	0
I	I	0	0	I	0	I	I	0	0
0	0	I	I	0	I	0	0	I	I
I	I	0	I	0	0	I	0	0	I
0	I	I	0	I	I	0	I	0	0
I	0	0	I	0	I	0	0	I	I
0	0	I	0	I	0	I	I	0	I

page 15
(1) AT
(2) CAT
(3) CHAT
(4) CHEAT
(5) CHALET
(6) ETHICAL

page 16
SP on SOR = SPONSOR

page 17
AWESOME

page 18

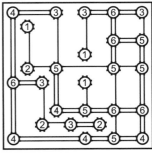

page 19
FURNITURE

page 20

9	8	7	4	6	2	5	3	1
3	1	6	8	9	5	4	7	2
2	5	4	1	7	3	6	8	9
6	2	3	7	1	8	9	4	5
8	7	1	5	4	9	2	6	3
5	4	9	3	2	6	8	1	7
1	6	5	2	8	7	3	9	4
7	3	8	9	5	4	1	2	6
4	9	2	6	3	1	7	5	8

page 21
SIGMUND FREUD
MORPHINE

page 22
SKIMMER
BLENDER

page 23
Ski 5. All the other skis have a counterpart with which the colors of the logo are swapped: 1-6, 2-4, 3-7.

page 24

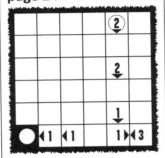

page 25
BANKERS
CHAPERONE

page 26

I	O	I	I	O	O	I	O	I	O
O	I	O	I	O	I	O	I	I	O
I	O	I	O	I	O	O	I	O	I
O	I	O	O	I	O	I	O	I	I
O	O	I	I	O	I	O	I	I	O
I	O	O	I	I	O	I	O	O	I
O	I	I	O	O	I	I	O	O	I
I	O	O	I	O	I	O	I	I	O
I	I	O	O	I	O	I	O	O	I
O	I	I	O	I	I	O	I	O	O

page 27
(1) BE
(2) BED
(3) DEBT
(4) DEBUT
(5) BUSTED
(6) DUMBEST

page 28
HALF WAY = HALFWAY

page 29
TABLOID

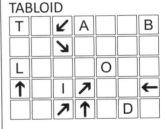

page 30

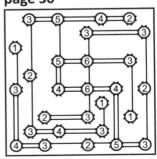

page 31
INSECTS

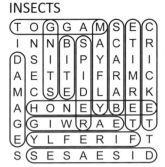

page 32

2	5	6	8	1	7	4	3	9
4	1	8	6	9	3	7	5	2
3	9	7	2	4	5	8	6	1
9	6	5	7	2	8	1	4	3
7	3	1	9	5	4	2	8	6
8	2	4	3	6	1	9	7	5
1	8	9	5	7	6	3	2	4
6	7	2	4	3	9	5	1	8
5	4	3	1	8	2	6	9	7

page 33
SCHOOLTEACHER
SMARTPHONE

page 34
SQUARE
PYRAMID

page 35
6. The difference in the scores forms the following series: -2, +4, -6, +8. Alternating per column, you also see the following two series: 7-14-21-28 and 9-18-27-36.

page 36

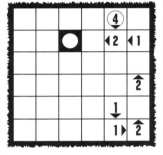

page 37
TELECOM
INFECTION

page 38

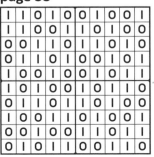

page 39
(1) AC
(2) ARC
(3) ORCA
(4) ROACH
(5) CHORAL
(6) CHOLERA

page 40
TH under CLOUD =
THUNDERCLOUD

page 41
OUTRAGE

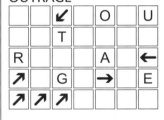

page 42

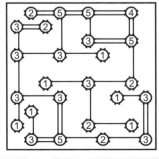

page 43
WATER

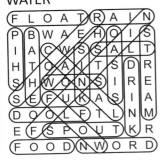

page 44

8	7	9	2	6	3	5	1	4
3	5	1	9	8	4	6	2	7
6	2	4	1	7	5	8	3	9
1	8	3	5	4	6	7	9	2
5	6	7	3	2	9	4	8	1
9	4	2	7	1	8	3	6	5
7	1	6	8	5	2	9	4	3
2	9	8	4	3	7	1	5	6
4	3	5	6	9	1	2	7	8

page 45
VINEYARD
AUSTRALIA

page 46
COTTON
LEATHER

page 47
From nine
different cakes.

page 48

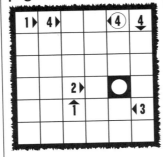

page 49
INHALER
BADMINTON

page 50

I	0	0	I	0	I	0	I	I	0
0	I	0	I	I	0	0	I	I	0
I	0	I	0	I	0	I	0	0	I
0	I	I	0	0	I	0	I	I	0
I	0	0	I	I	0	I	I	0	0
0	I	I	0	I	0	I	0	0	I
I	0	0	I	0	I	0	0	I	I
0	I	I	0	I	I	0	I	0	0
0	I	0	I	0	0	I	0	I	I
I	0	I	0	0	I	I	0	0	I

page 51
(1) DM
(2) DIM
(3) MAID
(4) MEDIA
(5) DIADEM
(6) ADMIRED

page 52
AIRLINE

page 53
CLINTON

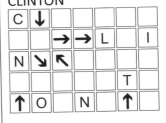

page 54

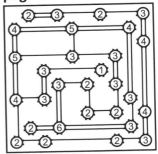

page 55
INTERNET

page 56

4	3	2	9	7	8	5	6	1
6	5	1	2	4	3	7	8	9
9	8	7	5	1	6	2	3	4
5	9	6	1	2	7	3	4	8
2	1	8	6	3	4	9	7	5
7	4	3	8	9	5	1	2	6
1	6	5	3	8	2	4	9	7
3	7	9	4	6	1	8	5	2
8	2	4	7	5	9	6	1	3

page 57
SALMONELLA
SOLAR PANEL

page 58
BLOCKS
PUZZLES

page 59
Vu. Read each word as three sequential letters from right to left.

page 60

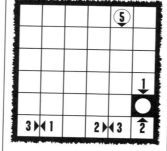

page 61
CHOLERA
IGNORANCE

page 62

I	O	I	I	O	O	I	O	I	O
O	I	O	I	O	I	O	I	I	O
I	O	I	O	I	O	O	I	O	I
O	I	O	O	I	O	I	O	I	I
O	O	I	I	O	I	O	I	I	O
I	O	O	I	I	O	I	O	O	I
O	I	I	O	O	I	O	I	O	I
I	I	O	O	I	O	I	O	I	O
I	O	O	I	O	I	I	O	O	I
O	I	I	O	I	I	O	I	O	O

page 63
(1) SE
(2) SET
(3) NEST
(4) INSET
(5) TENNIS
(6) INTENSE

page 64
COUNTDOWN

page 65
VAMPIRE

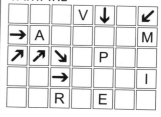

page 66

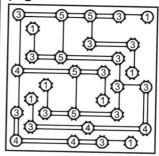

page 67
HEALTH

page 68

9	8	3	2	5	7	1	6	4
6	7	4	3	9	1	5	8	2
5	2	1	8	4	6	3	7	9
3	1	6	7	8	9	4	2	5
2	5	8	4	1	3	6	9	7
4	9	7	6	2	5	8	1	3
8	6	5	9	3	2	7	4	1
7	3	2	1	6	4	9	5	8
1	4	9	5	7	8	2	3	6

page 69
LOS ANGELES
ACCOUNTANT

page 70
BLOSSOM
COMPOST

page 71
Fiberglass cable 2. It has the equivalent of 15.5 glass fibers.

page 72

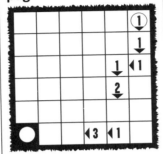

page 73
SINCERE
ARMCHAIR

page 74

I	0	I	0	I	0	I	0	0	I
0	I	0	0	I	I	0	0	I	I
0	0	I	I	0	I	0	I	I	0
I	I	0	I	0	0	I	0	0	I
0	I	0	0	I	I	0	I	I	0
I	0	I	I	0	0	I	I	0	0
0	0	I	0	0	I	I	0	I	I
0	I	0	0	I	I	0	I	0	I
I	0	I	I	0	0	I	0	I	0
I	I	0	I	I	0	0	I	0	0

page 75
(1) FA
(2) FAT
(3) FAST
(4) FACTS
(5) CRAFTS
(6) FACTORS

page 76
M on key = MONKEY

page 77
QUALIFY

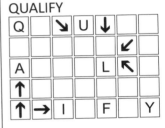

page 78

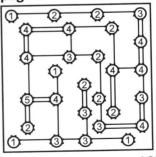

page 79
ENVIRONMENT

page 80

5	8	7	2	6	9	3	1	4
3	1	6	4	5	8	7	2	9
4	2	9	7	3	1	8	6	5
6	9	5	8	2	4	1	3	7
7	4	2	3	1	6	5	9	8
1	3	8	5	9	7	2	4	6
9	5	4	1	7	3	6	8	2
2	6	3	9	8	5	4	7	1
8	7	1	6	4	2	9	5	3

page 81
STEWARDESS
SPINAL CORD

page 82
BATTERY
OPENING

page 83
Angle 2. The doorknob is missing on the left side.

page 84

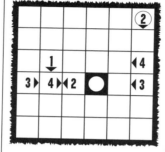

page 85
AMAZING
COALITION

page 86

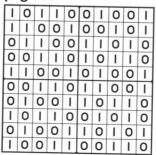

page 87
(1) E.G.
(2) GET
(3) GATE
(4) AGENT
(5) EATING
(6) VINTAGE

page 88
seven ties = SEVENTIES

page 89
ECOLOGY

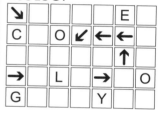

page 90

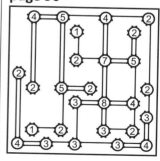

page 91
REPTILES

page 92

9	2	6	3	4	7	1	8	5
5	8	7	9	6	1	2	4	3
4	1	3	2	5	8	6	9	7
3	5	9	4	7	2	8	1	6
1	6	8	5	3	9	7	2	4
7	4	2	1	8	6	5	3	9
8	3	4	6	1	5	9	7	2
2	7	5	8	9	4	3	6	1
6	9	1	7	2	3	4	5	8

page 93
FOOTBALL PLAYER
MIDDLE CLASS

page 94
BAGPIPE
TRUMPET

page 95
Worm C. Eye color: black is dominant. Color on the body: gray is dominant. The number of body sections: four is dominant over five.

page 96

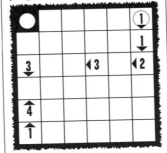

page 97
PIANIST
ROADBLOCK

page 98

0	I	0	0	I	0	I	0	I	I
I	I	0	0	I	I	0	I	0	0
0	0	I	I	0	I	I	0	I	0
I	0	I	I	0	0	I	0	0	I
0	I	0	0	I	I	0	I	I	0
I	0	I	I	0	0	I	0	I	0
0	0	I	I	0	I	0	I	0	I
0	I	0	0	I	0	I	I	0	I
I	I	0	I	0	I	0	0	I	0
I	0	I	0	I	0	0	I	0	I

page 99
(1) HE
(2) HER
(3) HARE
(4) HEART
(5) THREAT
(6) THEATER

page 100
WORKPIECES

page 101
ZIPPERS

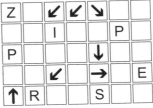

page 102

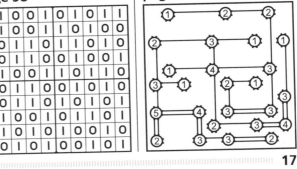

page 103
MATHEMATICS

page 104

6	8	5	1	3	2	9	4	7
3	4	9	6	7	5	2	8	1
7	2	1	8	9	4	6	3	5
2	1	7	3	5	8	4	6	9
9	6	3	4	1	7	8	5	2
8	5	4	2	6	9	1	7	3
4	9	6	5	2	3	7	1	8
1	3	2	7	8	6	5	9	4
5	7	8	9	4	1	3	2	6

page 105
HURRICANE
NEBRASKA

page 106
BOURBON
TEQUILA

page 107
Bell Bomnbimn. All the other bells have an *i*-sound and then an *o*-sound.

page 108

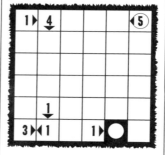

page 109
CABARET
INTENSIVE

page 110

0	I	0	0	I	I	0	I	I	0
I	0	0	I	I	0	0	I	I	0
0	0	I	I	0	I	I	0	0	I
0	I	I	0	0	I	0	I	0	I
I	I	0	0	I	0	I	0	I	0
I	0	I	I	0	I	0	I	0	0
0	I	0	I	0	0	I	0	I	I
I	0	I	0	I	I	0	I	0	0
I	I	0	0	I	0	I	0	0	I
0	0	I	I	0	0	I	0	I	I

page 111
(1) RI
(2) AIR
(3) RAIN
(4) IRENA
(5) AIRMEN
(6) CARMINE

page 112
COME
written backwards =
COMEBACK

page 113
SAFETY

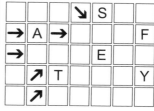

page 114

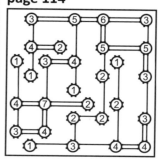

page 115
ACTRESSES

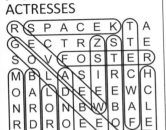

page 116

2	7	5	3	4	1	6	8	9
1	6	9	8	5	2	4	3	7
8	4	3	7	6	9	2	5	1
7	5	8	9	1	6	3	4	2
3	1	4	5	2	7	9	6	8
9	2	6	4	8	3	7	1	5
4	3	7	1	9	5	8	2	6
5	8	2	6	7	4	1	9	3
6	9	1	2	3	8	5	7	4

page 117
ENGAGEMENT
STATE TROOPER

page 118
HIPBONE
JAWBONE

page 119
Rose 3. All the other roses have thorns.

page 120

page 121
SURGEON
AGREEMENT

page 122

0	0	1	1	0	0	1	0	1	1
0	0	1	0	1	1	0	1	1	0
1	1	0	0	1	0	0	1	0	1
0	1	0	1	0	1	1	0	1	0
1	0	1	0	1	1	0	0	1	0
1	0	0	1	1	0	0	1	0	1
0	1	0	1	0	1	1	0	0	1
1	0	1	0	1	0	0	1	1	0
1	1	0	1	0	0	1	1	0	0
0	1	1	0	0	1	1	0	0	1

page 123
(1) LA
(2) ALE
(3) DEAL
(4) DELTA
(5) DETAIL
(6) DIALECT

page 124
disc over ING =
DISCOVERING

page 125
FORGIVE

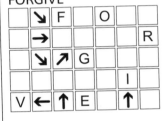

page 126

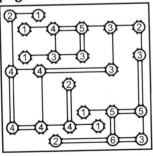

page 127
TOLKIEN

page 128

8	5	9	6	4	7	2	3	1
2	3	4	5	9	1	6	8	7
6	7	1	8	2	3	4	5	9
4	2	7	3	8	6	1	9	5
5	9	6	1	7	4	3	2	8
3	1	8	2	5	9	7	6	4
9	6	3	7	1	8	5	4	2
1	4	5	9	6	2	8	7	3
7	8	2	4	3	5	9	1	6

page 129
ELECTION
INDEPENDENT

page 130
CHOLERA
MALARIA

page 131
Candle C. Place the factors 1, 2, and 3 on the right colors; then add up each candle 5-6-4-6-6-7.

page 132

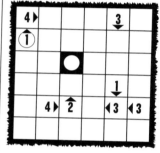

page 133
PALMTOP
RELIEVING

page 134

0	I	0	I	0	I	0	I	0	I
I	0	I	0	I	0	0	I	I	0
I	I	0	0	I	0	I	0	I	0
0	0	I	I	0	I	I	0	0	I
I	0	I	0	I	I	0	I	0	0
0	I	0	I	0	0	I	0	I	I
0	0	I	I	0	I	0	0	I	I
I	I	0	0	I	0	I	I	0	0
I	I	0	I	0	0	I	0	I	0
0	0	I	0	I	I	0	I	0	I

page 135
(1) ME
(2) EMU
(3) MULE
(4) PLUME
(5) LUMPER
(6) CRUMPLE

page 136
Z bra = ZEBRA

page 137
BALANCE

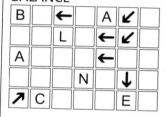

page 138

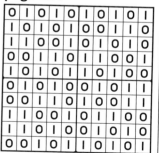

page 139
BASKETBALL

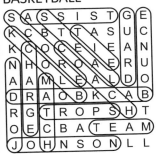

page 140

6	9	8	3	1	2	5	7	4
4	7	2	8	5	6	9	3	1
3	1	5	7	4	9	6	2	8
2	8	9	1	6	4	7	5	3
7	3	4	9	8	5	1	6	2
5	6	1	2	3	7	4	8	9
8	5	6	4	2	1	3	9	7
9	4	3	6	7	8	2	1	5
1	2	7	5	9	3	8	4	6

page 141
CONVENTION
NOMINATION

page 142
MANAGER
TEACHER

page 143
C5. There are sixty-five notes in total. You know there is one note too many and that the refrain is repeated eight times. Therefore, the refrain is (65-1)/8 = 8 notes long. If you compare every refrain, you notice that the note on C5 is superfluous.

page 144

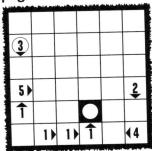

page 145
SANDBAG
BALANCING

page 146

0	I	0	I	0	I	0	I	0	I
I	0	I	0	I	0	0	I	I	0
I	I	0	0	I	0	I	0	I	0
0	0	I	I	0	I	0	I	0	I
I	0	0	I	0	I	I	0	0	I
0	I	I	0	I	0	I	0	I	0
I	I	0	I	0	I	0	I	0	0
0	0	I	0	0	I	I	0	I	I
0	0	I	0	I	0	I	0	I	I
I	I	0	I	I	0	0	I	0	0

page 147
(1) GO
(2) EGO
(3) LOGE
(4) GLOBE
(5) BOGGLE
(6) BLOGGER

page 148
MOS cow = MOSCOW

page 149
UKELELE

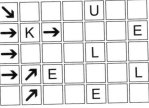

page 150

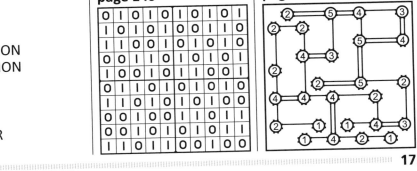

page 151
TOOLS

page 152

6	2	4	1	5	7	8	9	3
3	1	9	2	4	8	5	7	6
7	8	5	3	9	6	1	2	4
4	9	3	8	6	5	2	1	7
2	5	7	4	1	3	9	6	8
8	6	1	7	2	9	3	4	5
1	3	8	6	7	2	4	5	9
5	4	6	9	3	1	7	8	2
9	7	2	5	8	4	6	3	1

page 153
HUNTING
MARTIAL ART

page 154
GEARBOX
MIRRORS

page 155
14.51. The sum of the digits of the hour equals the sum of the digits of the minutes for all the other appointments.

page 156

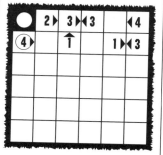

page 157
MEDICAL
CALIBRATE

page 158

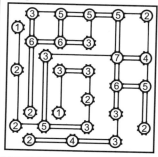

page 159
(1) PT
(2) POT
(3) PLOT
(4) PILOT
(5) POLITE
(6) TOP-LINE

page 160
strip T's = STRIPTEASE

page 161
HOTSPOT

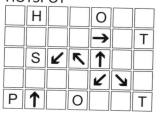

page 162

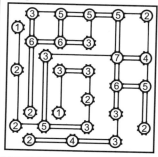